LUTHER
AND LEARNING

A group of the reformers. *Left to right:* Forster, Spalatin, Luther, Bugenhagen, Erasmus, Jonas, Cruciger, Melanchthon. From a painting by Lucas Cranach the Younger of the reformers and the family of Bürgermeister Meienburg, 1558. (Courtesy of the Staatliche Lutherhalle Wittenberg, German Democratic Republic.)

LUTHER
AND LEARNING

*The Wittenberg University
Luther Symposium*

Edited by
Marilyn J. Harran

SELINSGROVE: SUSQUEHANNA UNIVERSITY PRESS
LONDON AND TORONTO: ASSOCIATED UNIVERSITY PRESSES

Associated University Presses
440 Forsgate Drive
Cranbury, NJ 08512

Associated University Presses
25 Sicilian Avenue
London WC1A 2QH, England

Associated University Presses
2133 Royal Windsor Drive
Unit 1
Mississauga, Ontario
Canada L5J 1K5

Library of Congress Cataloging in Publication Data

Wittenberg University Luther Symposium (1983 : Wittenberg
    University)
    Luther and learning.

    Includes bibliographies and index.
    1. Luther, Martin, 1483–1546—Congresses.   I. Harran,
Marilyn J., 1948–   .   II. Wittenberg University.
III. Title.
BR323.7.W57   1983   001.2′092′4   84-40810
ISBN 0-941664-13-9

Printed in the United States of America

CONTENTS

FOREWORD

by William A. Kinnison

The faculty of Wittenberg University in Springfield, Ohio, viewed
the celebration of the five hundredth anniversary of the birth of
Martin Luther as an unusual opportunity for an academic community of its heritage. The institution that is the namesake of the
university of Reformation fame surely should undertake a special
celebration. Faculty committees organized a year-long program of
music, film, art, lectures, and traveling displays of the materials in
the University's extensive Luther Collection in Thomas Library. A
major emphasis was given to original works, including a traveling
exhibit of student art and the commission of a play and a music
drama.

But it was felt that the major celebration should be a focus on the
influence of Luther on the academic world. The result was the
"Symposium on Luther and Learning" out of which this volume
grew. It seemed particularly fitting that Wittenberg pay special
attention to Luther's influence on learning by inviting a number of
eminent scholars in the field to share their perceptions with the
students and faculty. The ramifications of Martin Luther's ideas
about learning have permeated the church and the academy alike.
He sprang from an age, not unlike our own, marked by controversy. He sparked a debate that shook ecclesiastical, social, and
academic institutions, and the tradition of Western education
clearly bears the marks of his influence.

Part of the genius of Luther was that he saw a learning society as
it emerged. "We are at the dawn of a new era," said Luther, "for we
are beginning to recover the knowledge of the external world." He

sought to bring scholarship and religion together rather than keeping them apart. It was the Renaissance, the dawn of the age of reason, and Luther and medieval Wittenberg were part of that great movement.

The authors of the papers presented here were invited to spend a week together at the Benjamin Prince House on campus in what became for them and for us an exciting week of debate and discussion and even argument by leading scholars between Luther celebrations elsewhere across the country. Their papers became the focal point for a week-long campus discussion. It was the opinion of those privileged to hear them that they were unique contributions to a better understanding both of Luther and of education and that this should be made more widely available.

The University is particularly grateful to the members of the committee who planned the year's events and the symposium. Professor Richard T. Ortquist chaired the Luther Committee, and Professor Richard P. Veler chaired the subcommittee on the symposium. Members of those committees were the following faculty and staff members: T. Edwin Boling, Edwin R. Brigham, F. Kenneth Dickerson, Charles A. Dominick, J. Arthur Faber, Kurt J. Fickert, M. Paul Hagelberg, Larry J. Houff, Barbara E. Kaiser, Robert O. Long, Bob Lee Mowery, Steven C. Reynolds, Roland H. Roselius, Kenneth L. Scheffel, John O. Schlump, and Michael D. Wuchter.

We also express our special thanks to Marilyn J. Harran of Barnard College who served as editor for her colleagues in the symposium and brought the work of six scholars to the point of publication.

William A. Kinnison
President
Wittenberg University

THE CONTRIBUTORS

Leif Grane
Professor Ordinarius of Ecclesiastical History
University of Copenhagen
Copenhagen, Denmark

Marilyn J. Harran
Assistant Professor of Religion
Barnard College, Columbia University
New York, New York

James M. Kittelson
Associate Professor of History
The Ohio State University
Columbus, Ohio

Daniel Olivier
Professor of Theology
The Catholic University of Paris
Paris, France

Lewis W. Spitz
William R. Kenan Professor of History
Stanford University
Stanford, California

Krister Stendahl
Bishop of Stockholm
Stockholm, Sweden

ACKNOWLEDGMENTS

A word of appreciation is in order to several people whose efforts have made the publication of this volume possible. Professor David N. Wiley, Director of Susquehanna University Press, and Mr. Thomas Yoseloff, Director of Associated University Presses, did much to expedite the publication process. Special thanks are also due to Ms. Katharine Turok, Managing Editor of Associated University Presses, for her work during the various stages before publication. Dr. Thomas Boslooper was an invaluable help in preparing the index and reading proof.

I am grateful to Fortress Press, Philadelphia, for their kind permission to quote from several volumes of the *Luther's Works.*

On several occasions biblical texts are quoted from *The Oxford Annotated Bible, Revised Standard Version,* published by Oxford University Press.

Since part of the work of preparing this volume for publication was accomplished while I was on leave during the spring of 1984, I wish to extend appreciation to President Ellen Futter and Barnard College for granting me the Special Assistant Professor Leave.

The last word of gratitude must go to President William A. Kinnison and his colleagues at Wittenberg University for their conviction that this book should be published and for their support and encouragement during its completion.

Marilyn J. Harran
Barnard College, Columbia University
October 31, 1984   Reformation Day

11

ABBREVIATIONS

LW   *Luther's Works.* 55 vols. General Editors: Jaroslav
        Pelikan, vols. 1–30; Helmut T. Lehmann, vols. 31–55.
        St. Louis and Philadelphia, 1955–1976.

WA   *D. Martin Luthers Werke: Kritische Gesamtausgabe.*
        58 vols. Weimar, 1883–

WA Br   *D. Martin Luthers Werke: Kritische Gesamtausgabe.*
        Briefwechsel. 15 vols. Weimar, 1930–1978.

WA TR   *D. Martin Luthers Werke: Kritische Gesamtausgabe.*
        Tischreden. 6 vols. Weimar, 1912–1921.

INTRODUCTION

by Marilyn J. Harran

In his excellent study *Luther: An Introduction to His Thought* Gerhard Ebeling asserts: "It is no exaggeration to say that never in the history of the university has the work of a scholar, in the study and in the lecture-room, had so direct and so extensive an influence upon the world, and changed it so much."[1] Such was indeed the case, and thus it is especially fitting that this series of lectures, given at Wittenberg University in Springfield, Ohio, in celebration of the five hundredth anniversary of Martin Luther's birth, be entitled *Luther and Learning*.

In many ways education was at the heart of Luther's manifold activities. Called to teach as a doctor *in Biblia* at the University of Wittenberg in 1512, Luther remained at that post until his death in 1546. His first efforts at reform were directed not toward the church but toward the university, where he battled to place Scripture and the Church Fathers at the center of theological study and for new attention to the humanities in the arts curriculum. Luther's younger colleague, Philipp Melanchthon, who came to be known as the *Praeceptor Germaniae,* worked diligently to institute these and other curricular reforms at the new university.

In the 1520s, as a result of his emphasis on the priesthood of all believers, Luther and his fellow reformers pushed for the revival of education on all levels, not only on that of the university. Luther literally unchained the Bible and made it available in a German translation that breathed the spirit of the people. He insisted that all people have the right and the responsibility to hear the Word of God preached and to read the Bible for themselves. Luther em-

15

phasized education as both a secular and a spiritual necessity for the welfare of all people.

Throughout his career Luther also remained firm in his convictions about what education can and cannot achieve. He resisted any effort to allow learning to become yet another form of works-righteousness. A person is justified by faith, not by knowledge; a person is saved through grace, not educational attainments. Thus, on the one hand, Luther wrote: "They are not the best Christians who are the most learned and abound in many books. For all their books and all their learning are the 'written code' and the death of the soul. But rather they are the best Christians who with a totally free will do those things which the scholars read in the books and teach others to do. But they do not act out of a totally free will unless they have love through the Holy Spirit. Therefore in our age it is to be feared, that by the making of many books we develop very learned men but very unlearned Christians."[2] On the other hand, he affirmed the absolute necessity of education as he outlined in his letter of 1524, *To the Councilmen of All Cities in Germany That They Establish and Maintain Christian Schools:* "Now if (as we have assumed) there were no souls, and there were no need at all of schools and languages for the sake of the Scriptures and of God, this one consideration alone would be sufficient to justify the establishment everywhere of the very best schools for both boys and girls, namely, that in order to maintain its temporal estate outwardly the world must have good and capable men and women."[3] While Luther was at one with the humanists in their emphasis on the study of languages, history, and the classics, as well as the Bible, he differed from at least some of them in his belief that education cannot of itself instill faith or establish a right relationship with God.

These observations suggest why it is especially appropriate that this collection of essays be entitled *Luther and Learning.* This title reminds us that Luther began as a reformer of the university, that his relationship with both the old and new learning of his time, scholasticism and humanism, was intricate and complex, that he did more than any other person of his time to transform education and to make it available to all, and that, finally, Luther himself became—even in his own lifetime—the object of study and learning, constituting in both thought and personality a fundamental point of discussion between Catholics and Protestants. Not least this title reminds us that Luther's own theological breakthrough, the so-called *Turmerlebnis,* occurred within the context of his research and lecture preparation at the University of Wittenberg.

The perception of himself as a person called by God to be a doctor *in Biblia,* a professor of Bible, was central to Luther's life. Against his will he was ordered to assume the professorship held by his mentor, the head of the Augustinian Order in Germany, Johann von Staupitz. Certainly when Luther took over the *lectura in Biblia* in October 1512 neither the town nor the university was regarded by anyone as being more than promising but still relatively obscure. Of the town Friedrich Myconius, Luther's friend, wrote in his *Historia Reformationis:* "Wittenberg up to that time was a poor, unattractive town with small, old, ugly, low, wooden houses, more like an old village than a town."[4] Even the report from Luther's enemy, Johannes Cochläus, may not be far from the mark: "A miserable, poor, dirty village in comparison with Prague, hardly worth three farthings; yes, in fact, it is not worthy to be called a town in Germany. . . . What would there be in Wittenberg were it not for the castle, the Stift and the University?"[5] Luther himself referred to the town as being *in termino civilitatis.*[6]

Increasingly, and especially after 1517, it was the young University of Wittenberg that gave the town its special character and fame. The university was founded by Frederick the Wise in 1502 so that electoral Saxony might have its own territorial university, the counterpart to Leipzig in Albertine Saxony. The very nature of its establishment foreshadowed the independent line the university was to follow. Frederick approached the emperor, Maximilian I, and not the pope, to ask for a charter to etablish the new university. Thus, as Maria Grossmann describes it, Wittenberg "became the first German university founded without the permission of ecclesiastical authorities and without recourse to the traditional benefices."[7] This independent character of the university from its very foundation played an important role in the futures of both the institution and the young scholar Martin Luther.

By all accounts Elector Frederick was both proud of and solicitous for his young university. He worked to attract the best faculty members and to establish a library. Apparently from its earliest days, Wittenberg was a place where scholasticism and humanism lived side by side. Unlike many other German universities, Wittenberg remained relatively free of the intramural warfare between members of the *via antiqua* and the *via moderna*. The official letter of invitation to the opening of the university, issued by Frederick and his brother John, also indicated that "besides the traditional subject matters, *humaniora* [were to be] . . . taught."[8] Among the very first members of the faculty were such humanists as Nikolaus Marschalk and Hermann von dem Busche, who, however, stayed only briefly in Wittenberg. Christoph Scheurl, who was appointed rector in 1507, remained in Wittenberg until he returned to his native Nürnberg in 1511. He did much to encourage humanistic studies, and, in his role as dean of the law faculty, drew up statutes for the university in 1508.[9]

The humanism that throve in Wittenberg has been termed biblical humanism. Although the term is problematical, as Professor Spitz discusses in his essay, it indicates a special emphasis on the Bible that came to dominate in the theological faculty and permeated the other faculties as well. The humanities, and especially the languages, were valued both as tools for understanding the biblical text and as worthwhile subjects in themselves. When Philipp Melanchthon joined the Wittenberg faculty in 1518 a new spirit was infused into the study of Greek in particular and the humanities in general. Indeed, Georg Spalatin, the chaplain and influential adviser to Elector Frederick, reported that he witnessed six hundred students attending Melanchthon's lectures in the liberal arts.[10]

Following the widespread circulation of Luther's Ninety-five Theses, the student enrollment increased at the University of Wittenberg, and the institution enjoyed a growing prestige. Not surprisingly, enrollments decreased after Luther was condemned by the Diet of Worms in 1521 and during his days of enforced exile at the Wartburg. Enrollments varied throughout the 1520s, but increased again in the 1530s. From 1533 to 1536 new statutes were formulated for the university under the guidance of the strongly Lutheran Elector John Frederick. With the passing of Luther and Melanchthon, enrollments again dropped. During the Schmalkaldic War, Wittenberg was captured by Charles V, but under the rule of the Lutheran prince Moritz of Saxony the university continued to function. Subsequently, Moritz's brother August and his son, Christian I, continued to support the university, although Christian sought to encourage the growth of Calvinism, and many Lutherans chose to pursue their studies in Leipzig.[11] Following Christian's death in 1591, the university regained its stature as the preeminent Lutheran university.

It was the Thirty Years' War (1618–1648) that presaged the end of the university. Because Germany was torn apart by war and Wittenberg itself was besieged, few people were able to continue their studies. The Seven Years' War (1756–1763) brought further destruction and disruption to both the university and the town. In 1813 the town was captured by Napoleon, and in the following year it was retaken by the Prussians. The end of Luther's university came at last in 1817, when it was merged with the University of Halle. The library was divided; the buildings were given to a seminary for training pastors. The original University of Wittenberg, which had from its very beginnings known so much excitement and innovation and which had been the platform from which several of the greatest figures of the sixteenth century, most notably Luther and Melanchthon, had spoken, had come to an end. In 1933 the University of Halle was renamed the Martin-Luther-Universität Halle-Wittenberg.

The story of the University of Wittenberg does not, however, end in Europe, in the Old World. Martin Luther himself was aware of the "New World" and spoke of newly discovered islands and land where the gospel had not yet been preached.[12] In the same century in which the original University of Wittenberg closed, a new Wittenberg University was founded in a new land, on a new frontier, once again *in termino civilitatis*. In 1844 a new college, named after the University of Wittenberg, held its first classes in Wooster, Ohio. Founded by the newly formed English Evangelical Lutheran Synod of Ohio and the Synod of the West, which included Kentucky, Indiana, Illinois, and Michigan, the college was established to serve the needs of young people living on the edge of the frontier. In 1845 the college was moved even farther west to Springfield, Ohio, near the main roads by which German immigrants were constantly on the move westward. The college, later constituted a university, remained committed to those same educational goals and values taught by Luther and Melanchthon, stressing the Bible and the humanities, and gradually adding those new fields of study appropriate to the changing times and needs of American students. Wittenberg University is today a thriving, modern institution, offering many fields of study in both the arts and the sciences.

The essays included within this book were originally delivered as lectures at the Martin Luther Symposium at Wittenberg University. The contributions, by three American and three European scholars, focus on the theme of *Luther and Learning*. The topic is one that bridges cultures, time periods, and confessions. Since Luther was the major figure in the curricular reform and emergence of the original University of Wittenberg and was the spiritual founder of the second Wittenberg University, it is especially fitting that these lectures on this topic were delivered there.

The opening essay considers one of the most important aspects of Luther's life, his role as a professor. His sense of vocation as a doctor *in Biblia* was crucial to his reforming activity within both church and university. Luther's affirmation of his own vocation was part of his new understanding of the importance and legitimacy of all callings and his leveling of the hierarchical distinction between secular and religious vocations.

Throughout his life Luther interrelated his roles as pastor and professor. In his pastoral activity he came to recognize the false way in which Scripture had been displaced by the preaching of indulgences. In his professorial role he struggled to place the Bible at the center of Christian life and study. His efforts to achieve this goal took the forms of translating the Bible into German, training theology students and pastors, and initiating compulsory education for both boys and girls. Through his affirmation of his calling as professor, Luther found the strength and courage to assume the obligations of reformer.

Leif Grane examines Luther's work as reformer and theologian in the light of his scholastic training. On the basis of a close study of Luther's early lectures and sermons, Grane argues that Luther did not contribute to the further development of scholastic thought. Indeed, on the contrary, from his earliest known work and throughout his career, Luther directed both his lectures and his sermons against scholasticism, both as a theology and as a method. Grane argues that the foremost impression that Luther made on his listeners at the Heidelberg Disputation was that of an anti-scholastic thinker. His anti-scholasticism manifested itself in his Ninety-five Theses and in his mature theology. Yet, at the same time, Luther respected the great scholastic thinkers, such as William of Ockham and Gabriel Biel, and compared his own contemporary opponents unfavorably to them. Grane's essay describes both the consistency and the development within Luther's theology. His anti-scholasticism led him to new discoveries and insights, but his purpose, that of placing the Bible at the center of theology, remained the same throughout his career.

Lewis Spitz considers Luther's intellectual development from another perspective, that of his relation to humanism. He takes the discussion far beyond the point upon which it so often centers, Luther's relationship with Erasmus and their exchange on free will. Within the general framework of the interrelationship between humanism and the Reformation, Spitz discusses three specific questions: How much humanism did Luther know? How extensive was his knowledge of the classics? What did humanism contribute to Luther's development as a reformer? Spitz's essay relates directly to the preceding one since he examines at length the issue of the ways in which humanism facilitated Luther's attainment of a solution to his personal religious problem—a problem in large part created and posed by his scholastic training. Spitz describes Luther as being both influenced by and promoting humanism. His essay persuasively demonstrates the complex interplay between Luther and humanism.

While Spitz's essay describes Luther's appreciation of humanism and the classics, James Kittelson's contribution, "Luther the Educational Reformer," addresses the problem of the tension that arose within the educational process between humanism and Lutheran doctrine. Kittelson discusses the tension that existed between the humanists' seeking of wisdom and the reformers' emphasis on doctrine, two goals that coexisted in Luther's mind but that tended in subsequent times to lead in very different directions. Kittelson draws special attention to the fact that the reformers, and particularly Luther, considered religion to be a matter of both the head and the heart. Religious knowledge was not simply a concern for intellectuals or professional theologians. In their efforts to inform the laity of religious matters, the reformers employed humanistic tools, particularly the *loci* method formulated so brilliantly by

Philipp Melanchthon, but for quite a different purpose than that intended by the humanists. Thus Kittelson's essay expands upon that tension between theology and humanism which Spitz discusses within the person of Luther himself. Kittelson notes the irony in the fact that Luther, who in large part affirmed the humanists' educational program and goals, responded to the religious ignorance he saw by producing catechisms, simple statements of doctrine. Kittelson maintains that in spite of genuine disagreements between theologians and pastors on the one hand, and humanists on the other, such as occurred in both Basel and Strasbourg, humanism and evangelical doctrine continued to coexist in Lutheran universities and academies. Humanist method was made, ironically, to serve doctrinal purposes. Ironically, too, Luther, who saw the person as whole and made no division between religion of the heart and mind, prepared the way for the Enlightenment with its distinction between the two—a distinction that continues to be problematical for modern Christians.

With the essay of Daniel Olivier we move to yet another contemporary problem, that of the relation between Luther and Roman Catholicism. Writing from his special vantage point as a Catholic Luther scholar, Olivier describes both the attraction Luther continues to hold for Catholics and the challenge he presents to the Roman Catholic framework. With the problems of modernity very much in mind, Olivier discusses the special contribution that Luther's theology can make in addressing them. He understands and presents Luther first and foremost on the basis of what is found in Roman Catholicism in Luther's time and ours. Olivier's essay is a provocative statement of how Luther relates both to contemporary Roman Catholicism and to modernity itself. Indeed, he asserts that it is the task of Luther scholarship to return Luther to cultural problems that were his and are still ours, and that his negative dialectic addresses so profoundly.

In the final essay Krister Stendahl reminds us that Luther was, above all, a biblical scholar. Stendahl describes Luther's fascination with the power of the word, and, like Olivier referring to the modern situation, he ponders the meaning of this emphasis on the word in the culture of the word processor. Stendahl describes some of Luther's special contributions, including the oppositional nature of his theology and his suggestion of a canon within the biblical canon. While affirming that these and other accomplishments give Luther's theology a special power and clarity, Stendahl questions how they relate to modern religious concerns. He asks, for example, whether the search for a center within Scripture can be anything but an arrogant one. Stendahl perceives Luther's special contribution to have been his assertion of the Pauline concept of justification by faith as the center of Scripture. Luther stated this concept with a power that illuminated an entire age and offered a new sense of Christian freedom while also recognizing that the Word of God cannot be narrowed or limited.

These essays offer the reader a sense of Luther's relation to the learning of his time, most especially scholasticism and humanism, and an understanding of his contributions to learning that affect us to this day, from his stress on the humanities to his insistence on compulsory education for both sexes. Yet these essays do not merely laud Luther's contributions. They pose critical questions regarding the effects of his theology and reform movement. They ponder the enduring significance of his ideas on the relation between learning and doctrine, his perception of theology as discontinuity, and his practice of seeing a canon within the canon. Perhaps above all, the contributors to this volume leave the reader with the awareness that Luther not only contributed much to make modernity what it is, but also continues to offer important insights in our struggle to deal with the problems of our time. As Olivier tells us, and as our world has come to realize so often, reason and power do not provide the solutions to our problems. As Olivier suggests, our foremost modern problem is fear, and learning cannot do much to resolve that problem. Yet Luther too lived in an age of fear—fear of the plague, the equivalent of our fear of cancer; fear of hell, perhaps the equivalent of our fear of a nuclear holocaust. He affirmed that only faith can free us from fear. All of his learning and all of his efforts to teach were grounded in that realization.

More than anyone of his age, Luther recognized the spiritual and secular importance of learning, while at the same time recognizing its limitations. For Luther learning was a joy and a responsibility. It was a joy to teach people both the Word of God and the great classics. It was a responsibility to see that they used their knowledge to glorify God and to help their fellow men and women.

Perhaps we may sense something of the very special relationship of Luther to the learning of his day if we recall that in his last written words, of 16 February 1546, two days before his death, Luther wrote of Vergil, Cicero, John the Baptist, and Christ—thus demonstrating until virtually his dying day his own unself-conscious reflection on both the Scriptures and the great classical writers.[13] If this blending of the sacred and the secular came to be a problem in later times, it was not one for Luther. For him, quite simply, all learning glorifies God. Perhaps then Luther would not be too distressed at the extent to which he himself has become an object of learning, at least not if we remember, even on the occasion of the five hundredth anniversary of his birth, to look beyond the man to the purpose to which he dedicated his life. As he said, "I shall be a doctor . . . and that name they shall not take from me till the Last Day, this I know for certain," and, as he wrote shortly before his death, "Wir sein pettler. Hoc est verum."[14]

NOTES

1. Gerhard Ebeling, *Luther: An Introduction to His Thought*, trans. R. A. Wilson (Philadelphia, 1972), 17.

2. *WA* 56: 338, 6–12; *Luther's Works*, vol. 25: *Lectures on Romans, Glosses and Scholia*, ed. Hilton C. Oswald (St. Louis, 1972), 326.

3. *WA* 15:44, 24–29; *Luther's Works*, vol. 45: *The Christian in Society II*, ed. Walther I. Brandt (Philadelphia, 1962), 368. Copyright © 1962 by Muhlenberg Press. Used by permission of Fortress Press.

4. Cited in E. G. Schwiebert, *Luther and His Times: The Reformation from a New Perspective* (St. Louis, 1950), 206.

5. Ibid.

6. *WA TR* 2:669, 12, no. 2800b; *WA TR* 3:314, 14–15, no. 3433. Cited in Maria Grossmann, *Humanism in Wittenberg 1485–1517* (Nieuwkoop, 1975), 36.

7. Grossmann, *Humanism in Wittenberg*, 41.

8. Ibid., 42.

9. Ibid., 60–75.

10. Schwiebert, *Luther and His Times*, 255.

11. Helmar Junghans, *Wittenberg als Lutherstadt* (Berlin, 1979), 143–44, 163.

12. *WA* 10/1:21, 14–17; *WA* 10/3:139, 20–21; *WA* 53:169.

13. "Sancta poemata Doctoris Lutheri. Vergilium in Bucolicis et Georgicis nemo potest intelligere, nisi quinque annis primum fuerit pastor aut agricola. Ciceronem in epistolis nemo secundo intelligit, nisi viginti annis sit versatus in republica aliqua insigni. Scripturas sacras sciat se nemo gustasse satis, nisi centum annis cum prophetis ecclesias gubernaverit. Quare ingens est miraculum primum Iohannis Baptistae, secundum Christi, tertium apostolorum. Hanc tu ne divinam

Aeneida tenta, sed vestigia pronus adora. Wir sein pettler. Hoc est verum." *WA TR* 5:317, 11–17; 318, 1–3, no. 5677.

14. *WA* 30/2:640, 16–18; *Luther's Works,* vol. 35: *Word and Sacrament I,* ed. E. Theodore Bachmann (Philadelphia, 1960), 194. Copyright © 1960 by Muhlenberg Press. Used by permission of Fortress Press. *WA TR* 5:318, 1–3.

LUTHER
AND LEARNING

1
LUTHER AS PROFESSOR

Marilyn J. Harran
Barnard College, Columbia University

Martin Luther, a young professor at the University of Wittenberg, little knew that his posting of Ninety-five Theses for academic debate on 31 October 1517 would lead to such dramatic consequences in European Christendom.[1] In his role as university professor and doctor of theology, Luther had already proposed changes in the university curriculum. In his view, raising questions about church doctrine and practice, as well as about the theological curriculum, was a legitimate aspect of his calling as professor. No topic could be more central to the theme "Luther and Learning" than that of Luther as professor. For Luther himself, it was his calling, his *vocatio*, as doctor of theology and professor that gave him the courage to stand before the reigning authorities of both church and state, the pope, Leo X, and the Holy Roman Emperor, Charles V.[2] In 1532, after many years of tumult, Luther could still proclaim: "God and the whole world bear me testimony that I entered into this work publicly and by virtue of my office as teacher and preacher, and have carried it on hitherto by the grace and help of God."[3]

During the years of struggle and divisiveness that followed the publication of the Ninety-five Theses, Luther was greatly comforted by the realization that he had in no way sought the role and duties of a professor. Against Luther's will and in spite of his vigorous protestations, Johann von Staupitz, his superior in the Augustinian Order, had commanded him to prepare himself for the doctorate so that he could assume Staupitz's own teaching position in biblical theology at the University of Wittenberg.[4] When Luther pleaded that this new and unwanted responsibility would surely be his death, Staupitz replied: "For heaven's sake, our Lord God has great works to be done. He needs smart people in heaven too!"[5]

Yet Luther's fears about the immensity of his new responsibilities proved to be correct. Sounding very much like a modern academic, Luther complained about his unending obligations in a letter to his friend Johann Lang written in October 1516—a year before the response to the Ninety-five Theses would lend to his life complications of which he had not even dreamed: "I nearly need two copyists or secretaries. All day long I do almost nothing else than write letters. . . . I am a preacher at the monastery, I am a reader during mealtimes, I am asked daily to preach in the city church, I have to supervise the study [of novices and friars], I am a vicar (and that means I am eleven times prior), I am caretaker of the fish [pond] at Leitzkau, I represent the people of Hertzberg at the court of Torgau, I lecture on Paul, and I am assembling [material for] a commentary on the Psalms. . . . I hardly have any uninterrupted time to say the Hourly Prayers and celebrate [mass]. Besides all this there are my own struggles with the flesh, the world, and the devil. See what a lazy man I am!"[6] Some of his obligations stemmed from his responsibilities as an Augustinian and a priest, but many of them were related to his role as professor. Indeed, Luther came to regard his multifaceted activities as preacher and teacher under the rubric of his duties as a professor.

In his scholarly research and preparation as professor, Luther undertook a reexamination of the concept of vocation or calling. In his many writings and sermons he did much to emphasize the worthiness of any vocation to which a Christian is called by God.[7] Luther asserted that God calls each person to a particular vocation. It is not the case that some are called, priests, for example, and others are not, but rather that all Christians are called to particular lives and works. The individual's calling is more than one to a certain profession or work. Vocation in the larger sense applies to one's special role in the family and in society, as well as in a particular occupation.[8] Thus, in the strongest terms, Luther rejected the popular medieval view that only priests, monks, and nuns experience a calling. He likewise rejected the perception of daily, secular life as unholy, as not part of one's divine calling and as inferior to one's religious life. Accompanying this false understanding of vocation was the notion that each person has the responsibility to perform holy works in order to attain salvation. Luther argued in his Ninety-five Theses against this works-righteousness that was grounded in a belief in the possibility of accruing merit *coram Deo*, before God.

Luther explicitly formulated the idea of vocation for the first time in his writings in his 1520 treatise *To the Christian Nobility of the German Nation Concerning the Reform of the Christian Estate*.[9] In that work he proposed the concept of the priesthood of all believers. The importance of this concept cannot be overestimated since it led to the radical horizontalizing or leveling of the hierarchical distinction between ordained priest and Christian layperson.[10] Luther taught that in baptism all Christians receive a *vocatio generalis* to preach and to administer the sacraments.[11] In this regard, all Christians stand before God with an equal calling to be priests. An ordained priest does not stand nearer to God or on a higher spiritual level than does his congregation. He is simply the one who has received a *vocatio specialis* to perform this particular occupation in his life—a calling that in no way places him on a higher level than one called to another occupation. The priest or preacher has a special office, not a different or higher estate.

A person's calling, which includes but encompasses far more than his occupation, comes through the people he encounters daily, those people who may unknowingly be serving as God's masks, performing the divine work by calling one to particular activities and deeds.[12] Indeed, it was in precisely this way— although Luther did not recognize or appreciate it at the time— that God through the voice of Johann von Staupitz called Luther to be a doctor of theology, a professor.

In his later years of doubt and even despair, Luther came to rely heavily on the fact that he had been called against his will to a task to which he did not feel himself equal.[13] When Luther's colleague at the University of Wittenberg, Andreas Bodenstein von Karlstadt, renounced his doctoral and professorial titles on the basis of a literal interpretation of Matt. 23:10, "Neither be called masters, for you have one master, the Christ" *(RSV)*, and took to calling himself "Brother Andreas," Luther retained his titles of office, not because he valued the titles in themselves, but because he firmly believed that God had called him to this office, titles and all.[14]

For almost ten years, from 1523 to 1533, the University of Wittenberg suspended the granting of doctoral degrees, largely because the reformers believed that the doctoral disputation had been corrupted beyond repair by the scholastics.[15] Luther, however, was delighted when the doctoral degree was reinstated because he believed that the presence of well-trained professors of theology was essential to the success of the Reformation.[16]

As a professor, Luther was deeply concerned with the quality of education that his students were receiving. Early in his career at Wittenberg, he recognized the necessity for reform of the university curriculum and believed that this reform constituted an essential step in the reformation of the church. In May 1518 he wrote: "I am absolutely persuaded that it is impossible to reform the church unless from the ground up the canons, decretals, scholastic theology, philosophy, logic, as they are now pursued are rooted out and other subjects taught. And I go so far in this conviction that I daily ask the Lord to let things so transpire that a fully purified study of the Bible and of the holy fathers will be restored."[17]

From 1512 throughout the rest of his life, Luther performed fully the tasks of both professor and pastor. He perceived no conflict between the two roles, but used the experiences and insights gained in the performance of the one to illuminate and influence the other. In the posting of the Ninety-five Theses for debate, the academic act of a professor, Luther was reacting to his experiences as a pastor. In his pastoral duties, Luther had encountered members of his congregation who believed that they need no longer confess their sins and could by virtue of a letter of indulgence proceed on the hour of their death straight from the tribulations of this world to the joys of heaven. In his reading Luther discovered no scriptural basis for the claim that papal intercession could release souls from purgatory upon receipt of appropriate payment. As the popular "commercial" went, "Every time a coin in the coffer rings, another soul from purgatory springs."[18] Thus Luther brought to the university podium his concerns as a pastor, and he communicated from the pulpit his exegetical discoveries as a professor. As one scholar has aptly characterized Luther's activities, his "sermons tended to be lectures, and his lectures, sermons."[19]

Two events frequently come to the fore in descriptions of Luther's career as a reformer. Even though the posting of the Ninety-five Theses was not a dramatic event, it is often portrayed as one.[20] The Diet of Worms, in contrast, was a dramatic occasion because a solitary professor chose not to recant but to defend his beliefs before the highest secular lords of the land.[21] By so doing, he faced not only ecclesiastical excommunication but secular ban, leaving him a wanted and hunted man, homeless and friendless, or so Luther thought at the time. Important as these two events are, the one in 1517 and the other in 1521, by focusing our attention primarily on them, we perceive Luther as fundamentally a reformer of the church and forget that Luther was first a reformer of the university. Luther, in fact, usually reserved the word *Reformation* for the reform of the university.

In early September 1517, some eight weeks before the Ninety-five Theses, Luther prepared ninety-seven theses for his student Franz Günther to debate as part of the requirement for receiving the degree of *baccalaureus biblicus*.[22] In this *Disputatio contra scholasticam theologiam,* Luther placed in question two fundamental ideas.[23] The first concerned the content of university education and was a strongly worded critique of the role of Aristotle in the university curriculum. The second involved scholastic assumptions regarding the human contribution toward salvation.

Luther stated the first issue in three consecutive theses: "43. It is an error to say that no man can become a theologian without Aristotle. This in opposition to common opinion. 44. Indeed, no one can become a theologian unless he becomes one without Aristotle. 45. To state that a theologian who is not a logician is a monstrous heretic—this is a monstrous and heretical statement. This in opposition to common opinion."[24] And, as Luther summarized the entire situation: "50. Briefly, the whole Aristotle is to theology as darkness is to light. This in opposition to the scholastics."[25] The study of the Bible had been displaced by the study of Aristotle and the scholastic theologians. Genuine scholarly investigation had been transformed into frequently trivial dialectic and debate. In concert with other, humanistically inclined members of the Wittenberg faculty, Luther pressed for the study of the languages essential for biblical exegesis, Greek, Latin, and Hebrew, and for a renewed study of the Church Fathers.[26] In a letter of May 1517,

Luther wrote his friend Johann Lang that "our theology and St. Augustine are progressing well, and with God's help rule at our University."[27]

With regard to the second issue, in a series of theses Luther attacked scholasticism's, especially nominalism's, emphasis on the human ability to contribute toward salvation.[28] Long before his debate with Erasmus about free will, Luther affirmed in these theses from 1517: "5. It is false to state that man's inclination is free to choose between either of two opposites. Indeed, the inclination is not free, but captive. This is said in opposition to common opinion. 6. It is false to state that the will can by nature conform to correct precept. This is said in opposition to Scotus and Gabriel. 7. As a matter of fact, without the grace of God the will produces an act that is perverse and evil."[29] In a thesis that was to become thematic for his entire theology, Luther asserted: "25. Hope does not grow out of merits, but out of suffering which destroys merits. This in opposition to the opinion of many."[30]

The theme that runs through the theses is Luther's rejection of the assumption that a person, through his own efforts, can prepare himself for God's grace. He sharply and fundamentally disagreed with the nominalist assertion that God does not withhold his grace from those who do the best that is in them. Luther had been trained in this theology, that of William of Ockham and Gabriel Biel, at the University of Erfurt.[31] In his later accounts of his early career, he reported that he had enthusiastically sought to fulfill the requirements that this theology had set before him.[32] His efforts to do his best in order to receive grace and his attempts by his own natural will to love God above all else had ended in failure and frustration. As Luther later recognized, this theology leads either to a false trust in one's own efforts to gain merit before God, a position of arrogance, or to an unending uncertainty regarding whether or not one really is doing one's best, a position of despair. It was in despair, and as Luther wrote in his 1545 *Preface to the Complete Latin Writings*, in anger, that he turned to the Bible, especially to Paul's Epistle to the Romans, in his search to discover what the justice of God really requires from man.[33]

The *Disputatio contra scholasticam theologiam* demonstrates the way in which Luther combined his personal, religious searching with his academic responsibilities as a professor. The theses reflect his personal quest to learn how a Christian is to stand before God in faith and righteousness. They are evidence of Luther the professor's active engagement with the theology of his time. The theses were also the response of Luther the pastor to the recognition that he was not alone in his doubt and uncertainty regarding salvation. Scholastic theology's false emphasis on man's natural ability had led many into despair and into disastrous efforts to gain merit before God.

The Ninety-five Theses follow naturally from this critique of scholastic theology. They focus fundamentally on the issue of merit. Luther perceived the efforts of his Wittenberg parishoners to procure salvation through letters of indulgence to be the direct result of the theology of his time which falsely emphasized man's own ability and responsibility to contribute toward his salvation. In Luther's eyes the Roman curia, if not the pope, had chosen to emphasize the concept of merit, and the accompanying idea of a heavenly treasury of merit, for its own financial advantage. At that time, in autumn 1517, Luther had no knowledge of the intricate financial arrangement that had been concluded among Archbishop Albrecht of Mainz, the banking house of Fugger, and the papacy.[34] Yet, even without this knowledge, Luther was convinced that matters had gone fundamentally wrong when the papal indulgence, carried in procession on a velvet cushion, displaced the cross, and when people sold all their goods, leaving their families penniless and in want, in order to obtain a letter that supposedly freed their dead parents from the pain of purgatory.[35]

In his very first thesis, relying on the exegetical and linguistic work of Erasmus in his edition of the New Testament, Luther questioned both the Roman Church's emphasis on action rather than faith as central to the life of the Christian, and the entire penitential system, which also focused on action, rather than on true, inward contrition.[36] The Roman Church had even gone as far as to affirm that within the sacrament of penance, attrition, sorrow for one's sins based on fear of penalty, what Luther termed "gallows piety," could be sufficient, could count as genuine contrition, true sorrow for one's sins based on love of God, if one purchased an indulgence. Thus, in the first thesis, Luther wrote that "when our Lord and Master Jesus Christ said, 'Repent' [Matt. 4:17], he willed the entire life of believers to be one of repentance."[37] Repentance is much more than simply doing penance within the sacramental context. One cannot limit repentance to a small part of one's life.

In the same way that the New Testament speaks of repentance and not of the sacrament of penance, so too do the Scriptures speak of the importance of contrition and nowhere discuss indulgences. As Luther proclaimed in thesis 32: "Those who believe that they can be certain of their salvation because they have indulgence letters will be eternally damned, together with their teachers."[38] In contrast to the church's emphasis on indulgences, Luther asserted that the true treasure of the church is not the treasury of merits but the gospel.[39] Following the gospel, not purchasing indulgences, should characterize the life of the Christian. Responding to the indulgence sellers and the false guarantors of salvation, Luther proclaimed in his last two theses: "Christians should be exhorted to be diligent in following Christ, their head, through penalties, death, and hell; And thus be confident of entering into heaven through many tribulations rather than through the false security of peace [Acts 14:22]."[40]

Although no one appeared to debate the Ninety-five Theses, Luther had sent handwritten copies to Archbishop Albrecht, Bishop Jerome, and various colleagues and friends. He was in no way prepared for the onslaught that followed, when without his knowledge and permission the theses passed through the hands of his friends and on to the printers, who found in them the sixteenth-century equivalent of a runaway best seller. In his 1545 preface Luther recounted: "I got into these turmoils by accident and not by will or intention. I call upon God himself as witness."[41] As he phrased matters on another occasion: "But God's wisdom is greater than man's. He put blinders on me, as one does to a horse when one rides him on the street."[42]

Through the performance of his duties as pastor concerned for the spiritual welfare of his flock, and through his obligations as professor entering into debate with the theologians of his time, Luther "by accident" began the Reformation. At the same time, Luther's critique of scholastic theology and ecclesiastical practice emerged as a direct result of his personal struggle to stand justified before God. In that sense his public stance emerged as a necessary, not accidental, result of his personal struggle and eventual insight. That insight—fundamental to Luther's life and theology—had the character of both a religious experience and a scholarly discovery. It was in the performance of his scholarly duties as a professor of biblical theology that Luther attained the insight that proved to be the turning point of his life and the cornerstone for the Protestant Reformation.

The *Turmerlebnis* or tower experience has been the subject of much scholarly writing and debate.[43] If it is true that more has been written about Luther than about any other figure in history with the exception of Jesus, then it is also true that much of the literature focuses on this particular event in his life. Many of the analyses have centered on Luther's 1545 account of his experience in the *Preface to the Complete Latin Writings.* In that account Luther was not concerned with detailing his personal experience but with outlining the course that the Reformation had taken. His primary interest was to report how he had been compelled by both God and the papists to take positions he had never wished to take. He would by far have preferred the quiet of his study to the tumult of the public arena. As he reported, at that time he had neither revolutionary nor even reformative goals. Indeed, he even considered himself to be a defender of the papacy.[44] Although he had already engaged in writing against indulgences, he was still troubled and unresolved regarding the question of how one comes to be justified or righteous before God. Luther's reading of the nominalist theologians had led him only to despair and to the eventual recognition that their teachings regarding the role of human effort in attaining salvation were only human ones and stood in direct contradiction to both the Bible and the early Church Fathers, especially the Augustine of the *Retractiones.*

Luther's biblical scholarship convinced him of the fallacy of these scholastic teachings. His personal contact with his parishoners and students convinced him of the dangerous impact they had on the human soul, leaving it falsely secure and unrepentant. Yet Luther the professor, who had lectured on Peter Lombard's *Sentences* and on Aristotle's *Nichomachaean Ethics,* as well as on Psalms, Romans, Galatians, and Hebrews, was still at a loss to know how one might be righteous before God.

Unlike the medieval mystics, indeed, even unlike Augustine in his famous garden experience recounted in the *Confessions,* Luther was not freed from his confusion and despair by a mystical vision or voice.[45] Instead, Luther's insight, as he described it, came about in an undramatic, unsupernatural fashion, but in a manner that had an enduring influence not only on Luther, but also on those who were to succeed him, the evangelical Protestants. His insight resulted not from the hearing of an inward or outward voice but from an arduous, painstaking study of the biblical text— indeed, from the careful work of a professor of Bible. Yet Luther's scholarly investigation was no calm, disinterested pursuit. Quite the opposite; it was an impassioned and committed search for the truth. As Luther reported in a famous passage from his preface, "I raged with a fierce and troubled conscience. Nevertheless, I beat importunately upon Paul at that place, ardently desiring to know what St. Paul wanted. At last, by the mercy of God, meditating day and night, I gave heed to the context of the words, namely, 'In it the righteousness of God is revealed, as it is written, "He who through faith is righteous shall live."' There I began to understand that the righteousness of God is revealed by the gospel, namely, the passive righteousness with which merciful God justifies us by faith, as it is written, 'He who through faith is righteous shall live.' Here I felt that I was altogether born again and had entered paradise itself through open gates. There a totally other face of the entire Scripture showed itself to me."[46]

Luther's insight included both a fresh perception of the nature of God and His relation to humankind, and a different understanding of Scriptural interpretation. He applied his manner of interpretation to other texts, finding them now to be illuminated in a new way: "I ran through the Scriptures from memory. I also found in other terms an analogy, as, the work of God, that is, what God does in us, the power of God, with which he makes us strong, the wisdom of God, with which he makes us wise, the strength of God, the salvation of God, the glory of God."[47]

The circumstances of Luther's discovery tell us much about his understanding of vocation and the way in which God addresses his creatures. For Luther there was no division between his occupation as a professor and his own religious life. It was within the context of fulfilling the obligations of his vocation that Luther reached the insight that was to change his life. He attained the answer to his questioning while performing the work of his vocation, not apart from it. The very nature of his insight meant that it was not limited to those few people who are professional biblical scholars. Luther's insight was experimental in the true sense of that word. The consequences of his conversion were no less dramatic than had been those of Paul and Augustine. Luther recounted that he felt "altogether born again and had entered paradise itself through open gates."[48] Dramatic as his experience was, it also occurred within the realm of the ordinary, within a context accessible to any Christian—in reading, meditating, and reflecting upon the Bible. From Luther's momentous discovery we gain a sense of the living Word, the living voice or presence of God, at work in Scripture. Luther's insight into the meaning of justification by faith was both experiential and experimental because it could be verified by every Christian who reads the Scriptures prayerfully and allows himself or herself to be addressed by them.

Since the Bible contains the living Word of God, Luther asserted that it must be accessible to all Christians. As Luther eloquently argued in his 1520 treatises, the Bible must be unchained and once again be the possession of all Christians. In his treatise *To the Christian Nobility* Luther condemned the position that only the pope has the right to interpret Scripture. He affirmed the right of every Christian to read and to interpret Scripture as central to the priesthood of all believers. Luther was convinced that the Holy Spirit enables each Christian to understand and to interpret Scripture accurately. When one passage appeared unclear, Luther advocated that a person should seek out another, clearer passage to help him resolve the unclear one.[49] The Bible is not a closed book, filled with secret knowledge and accessible only to a few, but an open book that clearly states God's commands, his acts in history, and his love through Christ for humanity. In his exegesis Luther gradually came to repudiate the traditional fourfold manner of interpretation, in which the mystical or allegorical meaning often predominated, and argued in its place for the historical or literal interpretation.[50] Because Luther had such a strong belief in the power of the Word at work in Scripture, he had no doubts that Christians could understand the Bible. Yet this understanding could not come to pass when Christians remained unable to read and when the Word was not preached in sermons.

In the Ninety-five Theses, Luther had already emphasized the overriding importance of the Word, in contradistinction to indulgences or any other matter. In theses 53 and 54 he wrote: "They are the enemies of Christ and of the pope who forbid altogether the preaching of the Word of God in some churches in order that indulgences be preached in others," and "Injury is done to the Word of God when, in the same sermon, an equal or larger amount of time is devoted to indulgences than to the Word."[51] The true treasure of the church is not indulgences but the gospel.[52]

In his vocation as professor, Luther struggled to place the Scriptures once again at the center of Christian life and theology. His efforts took several different but interrelated forms: in the translation of the Bible into German, in the training of theology students and pastors, and in the effort to initiate compulsory education for boys and girls so that all might read the Word of God.

One of those works of his career which Luther valued the most and in which he took the most joy was his translation of the Bible.[53] Since each individual stands directly before God, responsible for his own life and actions in the world, Luther recognized that it was absolutely essential that the Bible be made available to his fellow Germans in their native language so that they could learn for themselves the true gospel of Christ.

Luther began his translation of the New Testament during his enforced exile at the Wartburg, and his work of translating and revising came to occupy him until the end of his life. Amazing as it seems, he apparently completed the first draft of his translation of the New Testament in some eleven weeks, using as his working tools the Greek and Latin editions of Erasmus. Not only did Luther prepare a superb translation, a version that seemed fresh and alive because, as one scholar has phrased it, "he read Holy Writ 'as though it had been written yesterday,'"[54] but also, in the process of translation, he helped to sculpt the German language. The development of *Neuhochdeutsch*, early modern high German, was underway before the appearance of Luther's Bible, due partly to the influence of Saxon *Kanzeleideutsch* or chancellory German.[55] Luther's Bible brought new high German into the parish schools and pulpits and made it the common language for the German people, even though the common folk long clung to their individual dialects. In brief, the language of Luther's Bible "became the language of the people, the language used in the studies of the scholars, and the language spoken in the huts of the unlearned."[56]

Luther's careful study of the Scriptures in the preparation of his lectures had prepared him well for the enormous task of translation. In his activities as pastor Luther had also come intimately into contact with the people of Wittenberg. He recognized that the philological tools of the scholar must work with the language of the people so that the Bible would again become a living voice. The Word must be permitted to speak to the people in their own language—as Jesus spoke to the crowds on the Sermon on the Mount—and not be obstructed by faulty and unnecessary terminology. As Luther described the translator's task, "we do not have to inquire of the literal Latin, how we are to speak German, as these asses do. Rather we must inquire about this of the mother in the home, the children on the street, the common man in the marketplace. We must be guided by their language, the way they speak, and do our translating accordingly. That way they will understand it and recognize that we are speaking German to them."[57] Luther the translator, the professor laboring at his scholarly task of translating the Scriptures, balanced the demands of philology and grammatical and historical interpretation with the need to make the Bible a contemporary document for every German.

Especially in his work on the Old Testament, Luther considered himself to be only one of a consortium of scholars at work on the project. He was convinced that a translator should not work alone, for, as he said, "the correct and appropriate words do not always occur to one person alone."[58] He also knew that the process of translation often stumbles rather than flows along, leaving the translator at his wits' end and sometimes ready to throw pen, paper, and text out the window. That frustration emerges in this account that Luther gave of his efforts: "I have constantly tried, in translating, to produce a pure and clear German, and it has often happened that for two or three or four weeks we have searched and inquired for a single word and sometimes not found it even then. In translating Job, Master Philip, Aurogallus, and I labored so, that sometimes we scarcely handled three lines in four days."[59]

Even though the task was not without its difficulties, for Luther the professor, who had come to realize the centrality of the Bible to Christian life, it was a task that had to be completed. Luther once remarked that "translating is not every man's skill as the mad saints imagine. It requires a right, devout, honest, sincere, God-fearing, Christian, trained, informed, and experienced heart."[60] The biblical translator must be more than a skilled linguist, he must be a theologian, and that, as Luther well knew, is a vocation to which no person can bring himself by his own will and efforts. In a moving statement he once said, "One becomes a theologian by living, no, rather by dying and being damned, not by understanding, reading, or speculating."[61]

Luther also believed that the Bible should be at the center of the theological curriculum within the university. The beginnings that he made in revising the curriculum were developed and formalized under the able guidance of Philipp Melanchthon, who joined the Wittenberg faculty in 1518 at the age of 21.[62] Influenced by humanism, the new theological curriculum placed its emphasis on languages and history and displaced philosophy. Students were now required to study Greek, Latin, and even Hebrew, so that they could independently interpret the biblical texts. But the core of the curriculum was the lectures on the Old and New Testaments delivered by the professors of biblical theology. According to the statutes of the university, theology professors were obliged to " 'lecture an hour a day, four days a week, namely, on Monday, Tuesday, Thursday, and Friday.' Luther did not adhere strictly to this requirement, for sometimes he lectured more often and sometimes less often."[63] He appears to have lectured on the average two to three hours a week, but that, of course, was in addition to his manifold other responsibilities.[64] For ten years, for example, he served as dean of the theological faculty.

Luther, with whom we so closely associate the New Testament texts, especially the letters of Paul, lectured mainly on the Old Testament. In a university or seminary of today he would occupy the chair of Old rather than New Testament.[65] He preached mainly on the New Testament, but lectured mostly on the Old Testament.[66] Indeed, he was still engaged in work on his commentary on Genesis when he died in 1546.

All of these facts tell us much about the subjects with which Luther was concerned as a professor, but they tell us little about how his listeners, his students, experienced him. One of his students, Georg Benedict, offers a description of how those students who faced him across the podium at 6 A.M. in the summer and 7

A.M. in the winter perceived Luther: "He was a man of middle stature, with a voice which combined sharpness and softness; it was soft in tone, sharp in the enunciation of syllables, words and sentences. He spoke neither too quickly nor too slowly, but at an even pace, without hesitation, and very clearly, and in such fitting order that each part flowed naturally out of what went before. He did not expound each part in long labyrinths of words, but first the individual words, then the sentences, so that one could see how the content of the exposition arose, and flowed out of the text itself. . . . He had his lecture material always ready to hand, conclusions, digressions, moral philosophy and also antitheses: and so his lectures never contained anything that was not pithy and relevant."[67]

At the same time Luther was well aware that, like most professors, he could upon occasion stray from the point and perhaps say more than was necessary. On at least one occasion he had to appeal to his students for help since he had forgotten where he was in his exposition! In the preface to his Genesis commentary he wrote: "These lectures were delivered in an extemporaneous and popular form . . . mixed with German, and surely more verbose than I should wish."[68] If Luther managed successfully not to take himself and his own importance too earnestly, even when the lecture hall was crowded with four hundred admirers, he nonetheless took with the utmost seriousness his calling as a professor, that calling which he had never sought. He once said, "When I teach, it is not I who teach, but rather Christ, who lives within us."[69]

In yet another way Luther devoted himself to his vocation as professor. Luther's vast correspondence contains many letters that speak to his concern for the well-being of his students.[70] He wrote many letters pleading for financial support so that a promising student could remain in school. He also penned letters to students whom he knew to be ill or depressed. He even occasionally interceded with the parents of a student to allow him to marry. Certainly Luther was very much involved with the social, as well as the academic, life of the university.

He could also recognize with a practiced eye when students were making use of an opportunity to avoid their studies, as occurred during the numerous scares surrounding an outbreak of the plague. In one letter he ironically commented to Elector John Frederick: "I observed that many students have heard the cry of pestilence gladly, for some of them have developed sores from their schoolbags, some have caught colic from their books, some have scabs from their pens, others have caught gout from their paper. Many have found that their ink has become moldy. Others have devoured their mothers' letters and have acquired heartsickness and homesickness for their home town."[71] Nonetheless, in time, and in large part through Luther's efforts, theology students completed their training at the University of Wittenberg and moved into pulpits in electoral Saxony and eventually the other German territories. Through their labors the gospel came to be heard throughout Germany.

Luther the professor was concerned not only with university education but also with the schooling of younger people. He recognized and affirmed the importance of education on the rudimentary, as well as on the advanced, level, and his pedagogical concerns went beyond the strictly religious. In his letter *To the Councilmen of All Cities in Germany That They Establish and Maintain Christian Schools*, 1524, Luther affirmed that "now if (as we have assumed) there were no souls, and there were no need at all of schools and languages for the sake of the Scriptures and of God, this one consideration alone would be sufficient to justify the establishment everywhere of the very best schools for both boys and girls, namely, that in order to maintain its temporal estate outwardly the world must have good and capable men and women, men able to rule well over land and people, women able to manage the household and train children and servants aright. Now such men must come from our boys, and such women from our girls. Therefore, it is a matter of properly educating and training our boys and girls to that end."[72] Conservative as this proclamation sounds now, it was advanced and innovative for the time. Luther particularly underscored the necessity of a good education for those who would become secular rulers and authorities.

He remained deeply appreciative of those who follow the vocation of teacher. As he wrote in 1530, "I will simply say briefly that a diligent and upright schoolmaster or teacher, or anyone who faithfully trains and teaches boys, can never be adequately rewarded or repaid with any amount of money. . . . If I could leave the preaching office and my other duties, or had to do so, there is no other office I would rather have than that of schoolmaster or teacher of boys; for I know that next to that of preaching, this is the best, greatest, and most useful office there is. Indeed, I scarcely know which one of the two is the better."[73]

Luther's vocation as a professor, as *doctor in Biblia*, led him to act as reformer of both university and church. Convinced that God had called him to be a professor and doctor of theology, Luther spoke out against the ecclesiastical abuses of his time and dedicated himself to the cause of restoring the Bible to the center of both theological education and parish life. In the performance of his vocation Luther attained his fundamental insight into the meaning of justification by faith. In commitment to that vocation he struggled to make the cross of Christ once again the heart of Christian preaching and teaching. Although he had initially protested against his calling as professor, he came to see his vocation—and indeed, all vocations—as divine gifts and responsibilities.

Luther's own belief that God had called him to a specific occupation and vocation as professor gave him the courage to confront the secular and ecclesiastical authorities of his time. When his enemies and the voice of doubt within him questioned, "Can you alone be right?", Luther laid claim to the vocation to which he had been called against his will and choice. In 1530, after many years of turmoil within the Reformation, Luther still proclaimed: "I shall be a doctor . . . and that name they shall not take from me till the Last Day, this I know for certain."[74] Two years later, in 1532, he pronounced: "I have often said and still say, I would not exchange my doctor's degree for all the world's gold. For I would surely in the long run lose courage and fall into despair if . . . I had undertaken these great and serious matters without call or commission."[75]

Within the concept of vocation freedom and obligation exist in dynamic tension. On 31 October 1517, a young professor, fulfilling the demands of his vocation, posted Ninety-five Theses for academic debate—a debate that would lead eventually to the transformation of both university and church. Guided by conscience and belief in his God-given vocation, Luther stood before the Diet of Worms in 1521 and declared: "I am bound by the Scriptures I have quoted and my conscience is captive to the Word of God. I cannot and will not retract anything, since it is neither safe nor right to go against conscience . . . may God help me. Amen."[76] Luther's stand at Worms brought to a conclusion the first phase of the Reformation. By the words he spoke on that occasion Luther himself stood faithful to his dual vocation as Christian and as professor.

NOTES

1. There has been much scholarly discussion concerning both the content of the Ninety-five Theses and whether or not Luther posted them on the door of the Castle Church. See especially, Erwin Iserloh, *The Theses Were Not Posted: Luther Between Reform and Reformation*, trans. Jared Wicks (Boston, 1968); Kurt Aland, ed., *Martin Luther's 95 Theses With the Pertinent Documents from the History of the Reformation*, trans. P. J. Schroeder (St. Louis, 1967); Klemens Honselmann, *Urfassung und Drucke der Ablassthesen Martin Luthers und ihre Veröffentlichung* (Paderborn, 1966); and Heinrich Bornkamm, *Thesen und Thesenanschlag Luthers: Geschehen und Bedeutung* (Berlin, 1967).

2. On Luther's understanding of his calling, see Johannes Ficker, *Luther als Professor* (Halle, 1928), and Siegfried Freiherr von Scheurl, "Martin Luthers Doktoreid," *Zeitschrift für bayerische Kirchengeschichte* 32 (1963): 46–52. On Luther the professor, see Theodore G. Tappert, "Luther in his Academic Role," in Theodore G. Tappert, Willem J. Kooiman, and Lowell C. Green, *The Mature Luther: Martin Luther Lectures*, vol. 3 (Decorah, Iowa, 1959), 3–55.

3. WA 30/3: 522, 5–8; *Luther's Works*, vol. 40: *Church and Ministry II*, ed. Conrad Bergendoff (Philadelphia, 1958), *Infiltrating and Clandestine Preachers* (1532), 388. Copyright © 1958 by Fortress Press. Used by permission. See also Harold J. Grimm, *Martin Luther as a Preacher* (Columbus, Ohio, 1929).

4. From 1503 until his resignation in 1520, Staupitz served as vicar-general of the Reformed Congregation of the Hermits of St. Augustine in Germany. On Staupitz and his theology, see David C. Steinmetz, *Misericordia Dei: The Theology of Johannes von Staupitz in Its Late Medieval Setting* (Leiden, 1968), and *Luther and Stauptiz: An Essay in the Intellectual Origins of the Protestant Reformation* (Durham, N.C., 1980).

5. *WA TR* 3: 188, 18–19, no. 3134b.

6. *WA Br* 1: 72, 4–13, no. 28 (26 October 1516); *Luther's Works*, vol. 48: *Letters I*, ed. and trans. Gottfried G. Krodel (Philadelphia, 1963), 27–28. Copyright © 1963 by Fortress Press. Used by permission. An excellent study of Luther's early theology and career is Martin Brecht, *Martin Luther: Sein Weg zur Reformation 1483–1521* (Stuttgart, 1981).

7. On Luther's concept of vocation, and the relation between station and office, and vocation, see Gustaf Wingren, *The Christian's Calling: Luther on Vocation*, trans. Carl C. Rasmussen (Edinburgh, 1958); Ruth Hinz, "Der Berufsgedanke bei Luther nach dem heutigen Stande der Forschung," *Luther: Mitteilungen der Luthergesellschaft* (1961), 84–94; Frederick Risch, "Der Berufsgedanke bei Luther," *Luther: Zeitschrift der Luther-Gesellschaft* 34 (1963): 112–21.

8. On Luther's understanding of marriage and the family, see William H. Lazareth, *Luther on the Christian Home* (Philadelphia, 1961).

9. WA 6:404–69; *Luther's Works*, vol. 44: *The Christian in Society I*, ed.

James Atkinson (Philadelphia, 1966), *To the Christian Nobility of the German Nation Concerning the Reform of the Christian Estate* (1520), 123–217. Copyright © 1966 by Fortress Press. Used by permission.

10. In his *To the Christian Nobility of the German Nation* Luther attacked the false division between secular and spiritual estates professed by the Roman Church: "All Christians are truly of the spiritual estate, and there is no difference among them except of office." WA 6:407, 13–15; LW 44:127; see also, WA 6:409, 1–7; LW 44:130.

11. Hellmut Lieberg, *Amt und Ordination bei Luther und Melanchthon* (Göttingen, 1962), esp. 132–34 on *vocatio generalis* and *vocatio specialis*.

12. Hinz, "Der Berufsgedanke bei Luther," 84–94. In his letter *To the Councilmen of All Cities in Germany That They Establish and Maintain Christian Schools* (1524), Luther suggested the possibility of differing vocations for parents and children: "The exceptional pupils, who give promise of becoming skilled teachers, preachers, or holders of other ecclesiastical positions, should be allowed to continue in school longer, or even be dedicated to a life of study. . . ." WA 15:47, 14–17; *Luther's Works*, vol. 45: *The Christian in Society II*, ed. Walther I. Brandt (Philadelphia, 1962), 371.

13. See, for example, WA TR 1:198, 3–5, no. 453; *Luther's Works*, vol. 54: *Table Talk*, ed. and trans. Theodore G. Tappert (Philadelphia, 1967). Copyright © 1967 by Fortress Press. Used by permission. See 74, where Luther is quoted as saying early in 1533: "Afterward the devil also speaks to me about this, and he has often tormented me with this argument, 'You haven't been called,' as if I had not been made a doctor." In his *Commentary on the Alleged Imperial Edict* (1531), Luther wrote: "However, I, Dr. Martinus, have been called to this work and was compelled to become a doctor, without any initiative of my own, but out of pure obedience. Then I had to accept the office of doctor and swear a vow to my most beloved Holy Scriptures that I would preach and teach them faithfully and purely. While engaged in this kind of teaching, the papacy crossed my path and wanted to hinder me in it." WA 30/3:386, 14–387, 1; *Luther's Works*, vol. 34: *Career of the Reformer IV*, ed. Lewis W. Spitz (Philadelphia, 1960), 103. Copyright © 1960 by Muhlenberg Press. Used by permission of Fortress Press. See also Heiko A. Oberman, *Luther: Mensch zwischen Gott und Teufel* (Berlin, 1981).

14. See Ronald J. Sider, *Andreas Bodenstein von Karlstadt: The Development of His Theology 1517–1525* (Leiden, 1974), and the volume edited by him, *Karlstadt's Battle with Luther: Documents in a Liberal-Radical Debate* (Philadelphia, 1978). See also the recent book on Karlstadt by Calvin A. Pater, *Karlstadt as the Father of the Baptist Movements* (Toronto, 1983).

15. Gustav Adolf Benrath, "Die Universität der Reformationszeit," *Archiv für Reformationsgeschichte* 57 (1966): 41. On the resumption of the doctoral disputations at the University of Wittenberg, see Paul Drews, ed., *Disputationen Dr. Martin Luthers in d. J. 1535–1545 an der Universität Wittenberg gehalten* (Göttingen, 1895). On the early influence of humanism at the University, see Maria Grossmann, *Humanism in Wittenberg 1485–1517* (Nieuwkoop, 1975).

16. On Luther's attitude concerning the awarding of degrees, see Tappert, "Luther in His Academic Role," 52–54.

17. WA Br 1:170, 33–38, no. 74 (9 May 1518). Cited in Lewis W. Spitz, "Luther as Scholar and Thinker," in *Renaissance Men and Ideas*, ed. Robert Schwoebel (New York, 1971), 87.

18. See Hans J. Hillerbrand, ed., *The Reformation: A Narrative History Re-*

lated by Contemporary Observers and Participants (New York, 1964), 32–53, for descriptions of indulgences and the controversy surrounding their sale.

19. E. Harris Harbison, *The Christian Scholar in the Age of the Reformation* (New York, 1956), 125.

20. For example, see E. G. Schwiebert, *Luther and His Times: The Reformation from a New Perspective* (St. Louis, 1950), 314–15. Schwiebert does note that there was nothing unusual in posting theses for debate.

21. Two particularly useful books detailing events leading to Worms are Gordon Rupp, *Luther's Progress to the Diet of Worms* (New York, 1964) and Daniel Olivier, *The Trial of Luther,* trans. John Tonkin (St. Louis, 1978).

22. On Luther's expectations regarding the theses and reactions to them, see Brecht, *Martin Luther,* 170–72.

23. WA 1:224–28; *Luther's Works,* vol. 31: *Career of the Reformer: I,* ed. Harold J. Grimm (Philadelphia, 1957), *Disputation Against Scholastic Theology,* 9–16. Copyright © 1957 by Muhlenberg Press. Used by permission of Fortress Press.

24. WA 1:226, 14–18; *LW* 31:12.

25. WA 1:226, 26–27; *LW* 31:12. Brian Gerrish, among others, notes that although Luther was highly critical of the intrusion of Aristotle into logic, he affirmed that students should continue to read the *Logic, Rhetoric,* and *Poetics* since they were useful in teaching young people how to speak correctly and persuasively. *Grace and Reason: A Study in the Theology of Luther* (Oxford, 1962), 36–37.

26. On the relation between Luther and humanism, see Brecht, *Martin Luther,* 160–63; 264–74, and Grossmann, *Humanism in Wittenberg,* 76–85.

27. WA Br 1:99, 8–9, no. 41 (18 May 1517); *LW* 48:42.

28. See Heiko A. Oberman, *The Harvest of Medieval Theology: Gabriel Biel and Late Medieval Nominalism,* 2d rev. ed. (Grand Rapids, 1967), and Leif Grane, *Contra Gabrielem: Luthers Auseinandersetzung mit Gabriel Biel in der Disputatio contra Scholasticam in Theologiam 1517* (Gyldendal, 1962).

29. WA 1:224, 15–19; *LW* 31:9. On the debate between Luther and Erasmus, see Harry J. McSorley, *Luther: Right or Wrong? An Ecumenical-Theological Study of Luther's Major Work the Bondage of the Will* (New York and Minneapolis, 1969). For a more recent but problematical analysis, see Wolfgang Behnk, *Contra Liberum Arbitrium Pro Gratia Dei: Willenslehre und Christuszeugnis bei Luther und ihre Interpretation durch die neuere Lutherforschung. Eine systematisch-theologiegeschichtliche Untersuchung* (Frankfurt a.M., 1982). See also Lewis W. Spitz, "Ideas of Liberty in German Humanism," *Church History* 31, no. 3 (September 1962): 3–16.

30. WA 1:225, 15–16; *LW* 31:10. For the subsequent development of Luther's theology of the cross, see Walther von Loewenich, *Luthers Theologia Crucis,* 5th ed. (Witten, 1967).

31. Brecht, *Martin Luther,* 33–103.

32. Luther especially struggled with the question of whether one is responsible for attaining humility as a nonmeritorious disposition for conversion. See Ernst Bizer, *Fides ex auditu: Eine Untersuchung über die Entdeckung der Gerechtigkeit Gottes durch Martin Luther* (Neukirchen-Vluyn, 1966); Rudolf Damerau, *Die Demut in der Theologie Luthers* (Giessen, 1967); and my book, *Luther on Conversion: The Early Years* (Ithaca and London, 1983).

33. *WA* 54:179–87; *LW* 34:327–38, *Preface to the Complete Edition of Luther's Latin Writings* (1545).

34. *WA* 54:180, 12–14; *LW* 34:329. See Scott H. Hendrix, *Luther and the Papacy: Stages in a Reformation Conflict* (Philadelphia, 1981).

35. *WA* 10/3:343, 34–344, 17, no. 50; *Luther's Works*, vol. 51: *Sermons I*, ed. and trans. John W. Doberstein (Philadelphia, 1959). See especially Luther's sermon on Matt. 22:37–39, preached at Weimar on 19 October 1522 on how pilgrimages and other acts of penance should be renounced if love of one's neighbor so dictates, 106–7.

36. *WA* 1:233, 10–11; *LW* 31:25, Ninety-five Theses.

37. Ibid. Thomas Tentler offers an excellent discussion of contrition and repentance in his book *Sin and Confession on the Eve of the Reformation* (Princeton, 1977).

38. *WA* 1:234, 39–40; *LW* 31:28.

39. *WA* 1:236, 22–23; *LW* 31:31, thesis 62.

40. *WA* 1:238, 18–21; *LW* 31:33. See von Loewenich, *Luthers Theologia Crucis*.

41. *WA* 54:180, 2–4; *LW* 34:328.

42. *WA TR* 1:601, 17–19, no. 1206.

43. Bernhard Lohse presents an excellent selection of the various scholarly positions regarding Luther's *Turmerlebnis* or evangelical breakthrough in the book he has edited, *Der Durchbruch der reformatorischen Erkenntnis bei Luther* (Darmstadt, 1968). Both the foreword by Lohse and the essay by Otto Pesch, "Zur Frage nach Luthers reformatorischer Wende," offer helpful overviews of the enormous literature on the topic. Heinrich Bornkamm argues for an early dating of Luther's evangelical insight in *Road to Reformation: Martin Luther to the Year 1521*, trans. John W. Doberstein and Theodore G. Tappert (Philadelphia, 1946), 109–17. See also Robert Herndon Fife, *The Revolt of Martin Luther* (New York, 1957), 197–202. For differing views on the dating of the *Turmerlebnis*, see Lowell Green, "Faith, Righteousness and Justification: New Light on Their Development under Luther and Melanchthon," *Sixteenth Century Journal* 4, no. 1 (1973): 65–86, and Uuras Saarnivaara, *Luther Discovers the Gospel: New Light upon Luther's Way from Medieval Catholicism to Evangelical Faith* (St. Louis, 1951). Saarnivaara argues for two decisive experiences, one far earlier than the other. More recently, John M. Todd has also suggested two breakthroughs—the first, that which freed Luther of his guilt by a new understanding of repentance, and the second, that which gave him a sense of wholeness through faith. *Luther: A Life* (London, 1982), 74–79. See also my *Luther on Conversion*, which makes the argument for accepting Luther's own dating of the *Turmerlebnis*, 174–88.

44. See, for example, *WA TR* 4:25, 10–13, no. 3944, where Luther insists that he even wrote against Erasmus for criticizing the pope. Hendrix, *Luther and the Papacy*.

45. On Augustine's conversion, see Peter Brown, *Augustine of Hippo: A Biography* (Berkeley and Los Angeles, 1967), esp. 158–81, and Arthur Darby Nock, *Conversion: The Old and New in Religion from Alexander the Great to Augustine of Hippo* (Oxford, 1961), 259–66.

46. *WA* 54:185, 28–186, 10; *LW* 34:337.

47. *WA* 54:186, 10–13; *LW* 34:337.

48. *WA* 54:186, 8–9; *LW* 34:337. On conversion as rebirth, the "twice-born"

soul, see the classic study by William James, *The Varieties of Religious Experience: A Study in Human Nature* (1902; New York, 1958).

49. See the discussion by Jaroslav Pelikan, *Luther's Works Companion Volume: Luther the Expositor: Introduction to the Reformer's Exegetical Writings* (St. Louis, 1959), esp. 130–31.

50. See ibid., 89, and Gerhard Ebeling, *Evangelische Evangelienauslegung: Eine Untersuchung zu Luthers Hermeneutik* (Darmstadt, 1969).

51. *WA* 1:236, 3–6; *LW* 31:30. Todd offers a brief but helpful overview of the indulgence practice and Luther's criticism of it in an appendix to *Luther,* 374–78.

52. *WA* 1:236, 22–23; *LW* 31:31, thesis 62.

53. For Luther's thoughts and the problems and responsibilities of a translator, see *WA* 30/2:632–46; *Luther's Works,* vol. 35: *Word and Sacrament I,* ed. E. Theodore Bachmann (Philadelphia, 1960), *On Translating: An Open Letter* (1530), 181–202. See also Heinz Bluhm, *Martin Luther: Creative Translator* (St. Louis, 1965).

54. Heinrich Bornkamm, *Luther's World of Thought,* trans. Martin H. Bertram (St. Louis, 1958), 280.

55. See further, Sandra Mosher Anderson, *Words and Word in Theological Perspective: Martin Luther's View on Literature and Figurative Speech* (Ph.D. diss., Northwestern University, 1973).

56. Bornkamm, *Luther's World of Thought,* 283.

57. *WA* 30/2:637, 17–22; *LW* 35:189.

58. *WA TR* 1:486, 22–23, no. 961. Cited in Harbison, *The Christian Scholar in the Age of the Reformation,* 127.

59. *WA* 30/2:636, 15–20; *LW* 35:188.

60. *WA* 30/2:640, 26–28; *LW* 35:194.

61. *WA* 5:163, 28–29, *Operationes in Psalmos.*

62. See Benrath, "Die Universität der Reformationszeit," 32–45; Karl Bauer, *Die Wittenberger Universitätstheologie und die Anfänge der Deutschen Reformation* (Tübingen, 1928); Clyde C. Manschreck, *Melanchthon: The Quiet Reformer* (Nashville and New York, 1958).

63. Walter Friedensburg, ed., *Urkundenbuch der Universität Wittenberg,* 3 vols. (Magdeburg, 1926), 1:174. Cited in Tappert, "Luther in His Academic Role," 42–43.

64. Ficker, *Luther als Professor,* 5.

65. See Heinrich Bornkamm, *Luther and the Old Testament,* trans. Eric W. and Ruth C. Gritsch (Philadelphia, 1969): "If one could divide Luther's professorship of the Bible, in his time united, into two fields as now done, one would have to call Luther a professor of Old Testament rather than of New Testament exegesis. He devoted only three or four years to the New Testament out of his thirty-two year career as a lecturer, and all the rest was spent on the Old Testament." 7. See also Willem Jan Kooiman, *Luther and the Bible,* trans. John Schmidt (Philadelphia, 1961).

66. On Luther as preacher, see Grimm, *Martin Luther as a Preacher;* Elmer C. Kiessling, *The Early Sermons of Luther and Their Relation to the Pre-Reformation Sermon* (Grand Rapids, 1935), and Ulrich Nembach, *Predigt des Evangeliums: Luther als Prediger, Pädagoge und Rhetor* (Neukirchen-Vluyn, 1972).

67. *WA* 57:lxxvi. Cited in Rupp, *Luther's Progress to the Diet of Worms,* 44.

68. WA 42:1, 27–29 (Preface to the *Lectures on Genesis*). Cited in Tappert, "Luther in His Academic Role," 47.

69. Cited in Ficker, *Luther als Professor,* 24.

70. Lewis W. Spitz gives an excellent discussion of Luther's role as adviser to students and their families in "Luther's Social Concern for Students," in *The Social History of the Reformation,* ed. Lawrence T. Buck and Jonathan W. Zophy (Columbus, 1972), 249–70. See also Theodore G. Tappert, ed., *Luther: Letters of Spiritual Counsel* in *The Library of Christian Classics,* vol. 18 (London, 1955).

71. WA Br 7:207,19–208, 25, no. 2209 (9 July 1535). Cited in Spitz, "Luther's Social Concern for Students," 257.

72. WA 15:44, 24–33; *LW* 45:368. On Luther as an educator, see F. V. N. Painter, *Luther on Education: A Historical Introduction* (St. Louis, 1928); Gustav Bruce, *Luther as an Educator* (Minneapolis, 1928); Ivar Asheim, *Glaube und Erziehung bei Luther: Ein Beitrag zur Geschichte des Verhältnisses von Theologie und Pädagogik* (Heidelberg, 1961), and Harold J. Grimm, "Luther and Education," in George W. Forell, Harold J. Grimm, and Theodore Hoelty-Nickel, *Luther and Culture: Martin Luther Lectures,* vol. 4 (Decorah, Iowa, 1960), 73–142.

73. WA 30/2:579, 28–31, 33–35; 580, 19–21; *Luther's Works,* vol. 46: *The Christian in Society III,* ed. Robert C. Schultz (Philadelphia, 1967), *A Sermon on Keeping Children in School* (1530), 252–53. Copyright © 1967 by Fortress Press. Used by permission.

74. WA 30/2:640, 16–18; *LW* 35:194.

75. WA 30/3:522, 2–5; *LW* 40:387–88.

76. WA 7:838, 6–9; *Luther's Works,* vol. 32: *Career of the Reformer II,* ed. George W. Forell (Philadelphia, 1958), *Luther at the Diet of Worms* (1521), 112–13. Copyright © 1958 by Muhlenberg Press. Used by permission of Fortress Press. Debate continues over the exact wording of Luther's speech, whether he actually uttered the words "Here I stand." See Roland Bainton, *Here I Stand: A Life of Martin Luther* (New York and Nashville, 1950), 185, and Brecht, *Martin Luther,* 438–39.

2
LUTHER AND SCHOLASTICISM

Leif Grane
University of Copenhagen

Luther's attitude toward scholasticism is of critical importance to the theme "Luther and Learning." There are several reasons for this assertion. First, it is an established fact that Luther's own point of departure was in scholastic philosophy and theology. Second, when he first sought to draw public attention to his academic activities, he came forward as an enemy of scholasticism, not only as a method and form of theology, but also as the basis of the university curriculum. Third, when he became famous and indeed notorious through the Ninety-five Theses on indulgences, the ensuing contest was a continuation of the anti-scholastic campaign, which he had begun before the Ninety-five Theses. Fourth, even after the breach with Rome, Luther never stopped commenting on scholastic issues, partly because he rightly identified Roman theology with scholastic theology, partly because he never ceased to employ scholastic terms for his own purposes. These four arguments both establish the significance of our topic in Luther's own context and indicate some of the main problems connected with the topic. They thus provide the framework for our discussion of Luther and scholasticism.

Our knowledge of the University of Erfurt and of the Augustinian monastery in the same town leaves no reasonable doubt about the kind of education that Luther received there.[1] He was trained in the *via moderna*, probably of an Ockhamist type, at both university and monastery. The concept *via*, of course, is purely philosophical.

In our modern times of pluralism we easily forget that the concept *via* could not be used in connection with theology. The divine revelation, the proper source of knowledge in theology according to the medieval understanding, is above the human division of "ways" or approaches. We have every reason to believe that the teaching in the Erfurt monastery was Ockhamist, perhaps in the spirit of Gabriel Biel of Tübingen, but we know very little in detail about the content of this teaching. Even if we did possess more information, we would still not know precisely to what extent it was decisive for Luther's development. Only in the minds of scholars are students regarded as true duplicates of their teachers. Genuine students are not such copies, unless they are unduly dependent on their professors, due to tyranny on the part of the professor or to lack of personality on the part of the student. Certainly we should not draw immediate conclusions from a specific source of "influence," unless we find proof of it in the writings of the person under this influence. The only statement we can make with some certainty before studying in depth Luther's own works is that he learned to think in a scholastic way according to the *via moderna* and to master the subject of theology according to late medieval standards.

In order to avoid the pure speculation that will inevitably result if we regard Luther as the product of different spheres of influence, summarized under labels like "nominalism," "mysticism," and "humanism," we have only one rather obvious way to proceed.[2] We must read the sources, the writings of Luther, the lectures, the sermons, and the letters. From the earliest testimony of Luther's theology that we possess, the marginal notes of 1509–1510 on the medieval handbook of Christian theology by Peter Lombard, there can be no doubt whatsoever that we are encountering a scholastic theologian.[3] His way of arguing, his concepts, his references, in short, everything that has to do with method, is scholastic through and through. On the one hand, we have proof that Luther was under scholastic influence. On the other hand, it is not easy to see him as a true disciple of any specific medieval theologian. Luther certainly reveals himself as an adherent of the *via moderna*, and he used terms and arguments that are typical of the Ockhamist school, but he is not at all easy to pin down. For instance, in the marginal notes to the *Sentences,* he was obviously thinking about the freedom of the human will along lines that are characteristic for the schools of Duns Scotus and William of Ockham, but his way of using familiar concepts is, if not original, then at least not derived from any other written sources.[4] In brief, there is no indication that Luther had literary sources other than some Scotist-Ockhamist commentaries to Peter Lombard, excluding, of course, the textbook itself, with its many quotations from the Church Fathers, especially St. Augustine.

The two sermons from 1510 seem to portray less of this picture of the scholastic theologian about to change the very setting of his presentation by virtue of his own special line of thought.[5] Since we are not concerned with conjectures about the way in which Luther came to this particular position, and we are unwilling by speculation to fill in the many gaps that the sources leave, it is advisable to proceed to the next stage, the *Dictata super Psalterium* from 1513 to 1515.

By becoming an expositor of the Bible through joining the theological faculty at Wittenberg, Luther became familiar with another theological tradition, exegesis. The significance of this change of scene, compared with the notes on Peter Lombard, cannot be overestimated. Whereas the practice of theological teaching based on the four books of *Sentences* made it natural to build almost exclusively on the scholastic commentaries, the exegetical tradition offered Luther immediate access to biblical exposition behind *and* beyond scholasticism—*behind,* meaning the Church Fathers; *beyond,* meaning the use of humanist biblical studies.[6] We cannot trace every step that this new reading drew Luther to take, but we certainly can observe a considerable change of mind in comparison with the notes on Lombard some years earlier.

There is reason to assume that not only the nonscholastic sources, but also the biblical text itself led Luther to ways of thinking that were different from those of the scholastic mind. Nevertheless, no reader of the *Dictata* can overlook the instances in which Luther's scholastic training comes to the fore. These passages are not frequent but they are very clear, and they testify to

Luther's original adherence to scholasticism of an Ockhamist type.[7] Already by the *Dictata* Luther had discovered that the manner of speaking in Scripture is very different from the ways of expression in the philosophical theology with which he was familiar.[8] This awareness is probably the reason why he usually avoided scholastic arguments in his *Dictata* exegesis. When such arguments appear, they very often seem out of place, but their existence leaves no doubt about the type of theology to which Luther returned whenever it seemed necessary or advisable to use what we would call systematic theology.

If we consider the sermons from this same period, the scholastic mode of thinking seems to be more persistent.[9] This attribute is difficult to explain insofar as sermons, like lectures, are concerned with biblical texts. Two explanations suggest themselves. First, Luther remained more dependent on the traditional practice in preaching because he began his preaching career some time before he made the observations that led him to avoid scholastic arguments as much as possible in his lectures. Second, it may also be the case that he simply felt obliged to hold to the usual form as long as he had not yet made up his mind about scholasticism. Whatever kept him from a breakthrough in preaching similar to that in lecturing, the lectures and the study behind them did influence the sermons in content if not yet in form.[10] In these years Luther was on his way toward a theology that was to be incompatible with scholasticism in every aspect. I can, therefore, offer the following conclusions to the first part of this discussion.

The early literary material, including the *Dictata super Psalterium,* demonstrates that scholastic training of an Ockhamist type was Luther's point of departure as a theologian. The *Dictata* shows that he is moving away from a scholastic way of thinking. There is nothing in this early material to suggest that any specific literary source, apart from the exegetical literature and the Bible itself, was instrumental in this transition. The picture appears the same with regard to the content of Luther's theology, although we must also allow for nonliterary influences, such as the mode of life in the monastery or talks with fellow friars, especially Staupitz.[11] When references to systematic theology occur, they are of an Ockhamist type. Thus we have no reason to assume any development in Luther within the scholastic framework.[12]

In the *Lectures on Romans,* 1515–1516, the picture changes considerably. Scholastic theology plays a much greater part than in the *Dictata,* but on quite a different level. If the *Dictata* testifies to a certain alienation from scholasticism on Luther's part, the *Lectures on Romans* demonstrates his open hostility. In his struggle to understand the Pauline text, concentrated around concepts like sin, justification, faith, grace, love, and so forth, Luther rediscovered the scholastic doctrines on these subjects, but in such a way that he had to turn against them. His reading of some of the anti-Pelagian writings of Augustine, used as tools in his interpretation of Paul, gave him the necessary support to initiate a fight against scholastic theology in which he denounced it as both metaphysical and moralistic. Although the attacks are more vehement and elaborate in the manuscript than they seem to have been in the actual *Lectures,* if we can judge from the student notes published in WA 57, there can nevertheless have been no doubt about his meaning. [13]

When Luther established to his own satisfaction that the traditional philosophical theology conflicted with Paul and was consequently an obstacle to understanding the gospel, he could not simply confine this realization to his students in the lecture hall. He had to do more: to pronounce publicly his convictions. Only one means was immediately available to him. He could use the academic disputation as a way to take action in the appropriate setting, the university. It is typical of Luther not to take this step until he himself was quite sure, not of everything, but at least of the unfitness of scholastic theology as an interpretation of the Bible. He found his opportunity at the promotion of Bartholomäus Bernhardi in September 1516. On that occasion he made public within the university the results of his *Lectures on Romans,* just concluded. [14]

Among Luther scholars the issue has been much discussed, especially in connection with the question of the so-called "reformatory discovery," whether the disputation *De viribus et voluntate hominis sine gratia* is more or less medieval, whether it is still "just" Augustinian or already shows specific Lutheran traits. In my opinion this whole discussion misses the point, because it considers what was in reality an event as if it were merely a collection of opinions or ideas. It is *not* very interesting whether the ideas in

the disputation were original or not. It is the action and its consequences that count. The matter at issue is the way in which Luther
by his understanding of Paul felt compelled to act against the traditional theology as it was being taught at the University of Wittenberg.

The disputation was not an isolated event. From now on, one of
Luther's main goals was to fight scholasticism wherever he could.
He tried very hard to win over Usingen and Trutfetter, his own
masters at Erfurt, but failed in this attempt to give the new theology a broader base.[15] He soon had many adherents in Wittenberg. It is understandable that he was enthusiastic about Karlstadt,
who, in his theses of April 1517, was the first of the Wittenbergers
to attack in a public document the fundamentals of scholasticism.[16]
Luther was slower in his own progress, but in September 1517 he
was ready. He published the *Disputatio contra scholasticam
theologiam.*[17]

Luther composed the theses with certain chapters of the *Collectorium*, the commentary on the *Sentences* by Gabriel Biel, as the
main target. In addition to Biel, Scotus, Ockham, and Pierre
d'Ailly are mentioned by name. Luther's marginal notes to these
same chapters in Biel, written in a copy of the *Collectorium*, offer
us valuable insight into his preparation of the theses.[18] By this time
virtually the entire University of Wittenberg was on Luther's side.
His efforts to spread his views beyond his own town, however,
were limited in success when the new contest concerning indulgences, penance, and confession brought the intellectual world of
Germany into turmoil.

As Luther's actions and writings in the time after the Ninety-five
Theses demonstrate, the anti-scholastic campaign remained his
aim. Although through the amazing impact of the Ninety-five
Theses, he very soon realized his responsibility to explain the matter at issue in plain German to the people, the indulgence contest
did not initially alter his conception of his own task as a theologian.
In accordance with his calling as a doctor of Holy Scripture, Luther
saw it to be his duty to battle against any false interpretation of the
Bible. Consequently, when he concluded that scholastic theology
was perverting the meaning of Scripture, his aim became that of
completely destroying scholasticism. He struggled to attain this
goal not only by disputations, lectures, and writings, but also by

determined efforts to persuade the Elector of the necessity of a complete reform of the university curriculum. We can conclude, therefore, that the purpose of Luther's first public appearance was not the reform of the church, but the reform of theology and university. It may be added, however, that he saw such a reform as one of the indispensable conditions for the reform of the church, a goal for which so many longed. [19]

Certainly scholasticism had been criticized before Luther began his campaign against it. Humanist biblical scholarship quite probably served to confirm Luther in his antagonism. His reading of Erasmus's *Praefationes*, the introductions to the 1516 edition of the Greek New Testament, could very well have strengthened his confidence in his views. But the action he took—quite apart from the topic—was against the aims and spirit of Erasmus. One could even say that in the eyes of Erasmus Luther's very method of campaign was typical of the scholastic theologian and quite unsuitable for the Christian. However much Erasmus and other humanists had criticized or ridiculed scholasticism, Luther's wholehearted hostility was of a totally different kind. His animosity was grounded in an intellectual achievement that was entirely his own. As long as Luther maintained his stand, he was driven forward from step to step. There was no chance to compromise, as the contest over indulgences would very soon demonstrate.

What we must realize is the extreme significance of Luther's anti-scholasticism for his attitude along every stage of his progress to the Diet of Worms. This recognition is not only essential for the interpretation of Luther's writings in these years, but it also offers an explanation for his widespread success among the humanists.

The attack on the Ninety-five Theses in the spring of 1518, with Johann Tetzel, Johann Eck, and Silvester Prierias as participants, placed Luther in a new situation. No longer could he choose the topics of debate in the way he had previously done in his self-imposed campaign against scholasticism. In order to defend himself against the accusations of heresy and error, he was forced to make clear his principles of theological proof. He did so already in a letter of February 1518 to his bishop. He proclaimed that "it is shameful for a theologian to speak without a text."[20] This text should not be Aristotle's, which "they", that is, the scholastic theologians, use more than enough, but "our" text, the text of Scripture, canon law, and the Church Fathers.

In his answer to Prierias and in the *Explanations of the Ninety-five Theses* he maintained the same criteria.[21] Whereas earlier he had attacked scholasticism on an exegetical basis, thus rejecting not only the doctrines but also the method, as a consequence of this rejection he now considered every kind of traditional scholastic argumentation totally invalid in a theological connection.[22] By so doing, Luther did not change his own attitude in the least. He simply elucidated one of his presuppositions in order to make it a solid bulwark against attack. This strategy served to bring into focus the question of authority while the original issues of penance and indulgences were reduced to subjects on which the theological argumentation was to be tested.

At least until the meeting with Cardinal Cajetan in October 1518, Luther had no reason whatsoever to think of the struggle as anything other than a continuation of his own anti-scholastic campaign. This perception is confirmed by the fact that Luther used the opportunity of writing the theses for the Heidelberg Disputation, for the general chapter meeting of his order in April 1518, to proceed with his plea for a biblical theology in contrast to scholasticism. The audience in Heidelberg, which consisted not only of theologians from his own order but also of professors and students from the theological faculty there, gave him a welcome opportunity to promulgate his ideas in far wider circles than he had been able to reach through his correspondence with friends in Erfurt and Nürnberg.

The Heidelberg Disputation, with its frontal attack in the name of Paul and Augustine on scholastic speculation and moral theology, made a great impression on the audience. Among those who became very attentive to the friar from Wittenberg were the later reformers Martin Bucer and Johann Brenz. Certainly some maintained, as Bucer wrote to his friend Beatus Rhenanus, that Luther said openly what Erasmus merely suggested.[23] To Bucer this was indeed the most important difference between Luther and Erasmus. How was it possible to listen to Luther and find him in harmony with the great humanist? It was only possible if the listener found the general theme of Luther's theses to be the recommendation of the Bible at the cost of the scholastic doctors. To have heard this statement declared openly in the blunt manner of Martin Luther must have been so amazing that Bucer barely considered the doctrinal elements in the theses.[24]

Since Bucer must be regarded as an attentive and intelligent listener, this observation tells us something important, namely, that precisely the anti-scholasticism in Luther's ideas was perceived at the time as the most remarkable part of what he had to say. If this conclusion is true, it becomes very understandable that Luther's fight with Tetzel and Prierias did nothing whatsoever to decrease sympathy for him—indeed, quite the opposite. For what happened in the combat? Luther rejected any reference to the scholastic doctors as mere words, *nuda verba,* and demanded proof, that is, references to the Scriptures, the Church Fathers, or canon law. His ability as a polemicist soon gave him a name in humanist circles. At this stage, we can say that the confrontation was perceived above all as being one of method. Apart from his anti-scholastic polemic, very little was known about Luther who to that time had not published any major work. The frame of reference was very much influenced by the conflicts of Reuchlin and Erasmus with scholastic theologians from Köln and Louvain respectively. There was no reason why Luther's fellow scholars should not see his fight with the Thomists Tetzel and Prierias as a continuation of these earlier clashes.

This impression was probably confirmed when the *Explanations of the Ninety-five Theses,* written in February 1518, was finally published in August. The *Explanations,* Luther's first major book, concentrated on the question of theological argumentation and, therefore, on true and false interpretation of theological texts, above all Scripture. He insisted on the necessity to give account for faith, *rationem reddere,* but in order to do that opinions were of no use, and opinions were what Luther called all scholastic arguments not based on sound theological texts. It would, however, be completely false to understand this principle merely as a question of formal authority. When Luther accused the theologians of speaking *sine textu* he did not necessarily mean that they were not quoting Scripture. He also implied that they used Scripture against its meaning. In this sense the entire combat remained a question of the true interpretation of Scripture. The authority of Scripture disappears when it is interpreted in an ambiguous way. Not dialectics but grammar is to be consulted if we want to understand the Bible. If the *vera grammatica* is used, there will be no question of doing violence to the words of Scripture, because the words will resist any attempt to pervert them.[25]

By these ideas Luther became convinced, not of his own correctness, but of the true way to interpret the authoritative texts. In the *Explanations* he could choose those texts himself and had no reason to feel himself in conflict with the church. Tetzel, Prierias, and Eck could only serve to confirm his own views, for they were representatives of everything he had already for some time tried to defeat. All their objections to his arguments could be labeled unfounded opinions *sine textu.* At the same time Luther declared his readiness to obey the ecclesiastical authorities. He could do so because it was beyond his power to imagine a conflict between the unambiguous clarity of Scripture and the official voice of the church. At the moment when he discovered this frightening possibility, that is, at the meeting with Cajetan, he had already in his fight with scholasticism elaborated his ideas about the true interpretation of Scripture to such an extent that no word of power could make him retreat.

He regarded Cajetan simply as a scholastic theologian whose insistence on papal authority without reason or proof was powerless. Due to the campaign against scholasticism, he had reached a point where he could no longer be persuaded to forsake his principles. The fact that he quite consciously saw his action as the duty of a doctor of Holy Scripture and in that sense a scholarly matter became clear when Luther was asked to tell the Elector his response to the papal decretal of November 1518, about the merits of Christ and the saints as the treasure of the church. In his letter of January 1519 Luther wrote: "In our times when the Scripture and the fathers have been brought forward, and when it is asked in the whole world, not what is said, but why this or that is said, I fear, would it not only be unbelievable but also derision toward and an ignominious shame for the Roman Church, if I would accept a mere word and recant?"[26] With these remarkable words Luther held to the principles he had elaborated during the first round of the contest. These principles were won through the confrontation with scholastic argumentation and thus constitute a sequel to the original anti-scholastic campaign.

We need not dwell on the preparations for the Leipzig Debate or on the disputation itself. What happened during the spring of 1519 and in the days of debate with Eck is enormously interesting and of great significance for the following time, but it contains little new material for our topic. Just as Luther had impressed young men who were admirers of Erasmus during the disputation in Heidelberg, so he did again in Leipzig.[27] In the meantime the fearful possibilities of the now clearly ecclesiastical conflict had become obvious, but many humanists and other learned men seem to have thought along the same lines as Luther himself in his January 1519 letter. The new biblical learning was compared with the traditional way of argumentation, represented by the very able Eck, at the expense of the latter. As far as many of Luther's followers were concerned, his way of doing theology, that is, interpreting Scripture, was really more important than his specific doctrines. If this perception is true, it would also help to explain the doctrinal variety that reformed theology would display in such a brief time.

At least in 1519, when many of those who came to play an important part in the Reformation were won over to Luther's side, he was still known above all as the uncompromising antagonist of scholasticism, and as such he was appreciated. For Luther himself, however, it was more important that the consequences of his campaign, with an inner logic of surprising coherence, had led him to the point where he was obliged to break with the ecclesiastical authorities in order to remain faithful to his own ideas of a true theology. From this point on, the way to Worms was a direct one.

We must conclude that the ideas resulting from Luther's fight for a new theology in contrast to scholasticism remained his theological basis also after the conflict caused by the Ninety-five Theses. He certainly made new discoveries on the way, supported in doing so by his opponents, as he declares,[28] but none of them forced him to change his fundamental views.

The Leipzig Debate awakened and alerted some of the universities. Tradition dictated that it was the task of the universities to decide upon questions of exegesis and doctrine. The two universi-

ties to which the verdict on the disputation was left, Erfurt and
Paris, were reluctant to decide. Leipzig had no desire to oppose
Luther publicly; Eck had tried in vain to persuade his own university, Ingolstadt, to decide against Luther, but Köln and Louvain
were ready to act.

When Luther became acquainted with their action against him,
he was not at all impressed, but his obligation to his own university
compelled an answer. A formal condemnation by a university was
still considered a serious matter. The two faculties had acted completely in accordance with the medieval way of handling dubious
masters. After a short, but crushing, characterization of Luther's
teaching they listed a number of sentences as heretical or dangerous. This method had once been effective and uncontested, but the
condemnation of Luther was published at a time when academic
circles in Germany were no longer ready to accept this kind of
procedure. All adherents of serious scholarship looked upon this
type of scholasticism as an outmoded and useless method.

Luther's answer to the two universities' condemnation—and the
same applies to his later answer to the Sorbonne in Paris—
corresponded with the view he had taken in earlier polemical writings. He regarded the accusations as void of meaning and therefore
laughable, because no reasons or proofs were given for them. The
condemnation consisted of mere words, and no human institutions,
neither universities nor ecclesiastical authorities, are to be believed unless they render account for their statements. The radi-
cality of this standpoint goes far beyond that of any other critic of
scholasticism at the beginning of the sixteenth century. Any attempt to understand this difference by virtue of Luther's religious
seriousness or the like would be an offense to the intellectual
achievement of Luther's scholarship.

In the decisive year 1520, when Luther took the final steps
toward open war with Rome, he could hardly hope any longer that
a reform of Wittenberg University could provide a pattern that
other universities would follow. In most cases the universities remained scholastic until they eventually were reformed together
with the churches in their respective countries or territories. It was
the freedom of the university professor and the intellectual ability
acquired and strengthened within the walls of the university that

gave Luther the instruments to initiate the revolt leading to the Reformation, but, ironically, his colleagues at other universities were the last to follow him.

In the years 1520–1522 when Luther in a sense completed his battle against Rome and the scholastic tradition, he still had urgent need of his own scholastic learning. He utilized this knowledge not only in some of his conflicts with private persons like Jakob Latomus and Ambrosius Catharinus, but also in his critique of ecclesiastical institutions. Books like *De captivitate babylonica, De abroganda missa privata,* and *De votis monasticis M. Lutheri iudicium* would be unthinkable without a thoroughgoing knowledge of scholastic doctrine. If we take his attack upon the doctrine of the sacraments in the *De captivitate babylonica* as an example, we see that Luther not only criticized scholastic opinions, but also used the differences between the medieval schools to his own advantage. Concerning the doctrine of transubstantiation, for instance, Luther turned against Thomas Aquinas by employing Ockhamist criticism. A certain amount of school pride may also have been present when Luther ridiculed the interpretation of Aristotle by Thomas, but his main purpose was to use Pierre d'Ailly as a weapon with which to destroy Thomas.[29] Some Luther scholars may have been led astray when Luther professed that he felt sympathy for the doctrine of consubstantiation, but it would be completely wrong to interpret Luther's own doctrine of the eucharist according to the Aristotelian category of substance.[30] Luther used d'Ailly to throw doubt on the theory of transubstantiation as a *doctrine.*

Although Luther soon became involved in conflicts with people from the evangelical camp, scholasticism remained in his eyes the most serious enemy. In his academic lectures, where polemics were not the main concern although often a necessary part of his interpretation, Luther constantly attacked scholastic doctrines. He told Erasmus and Zwingli that they were poor opponents compared with the scholastic theologians. It would therefore be wrong to understand Luther's antagonism toward scholasticism as lack of respect. On the contrary, he considered scholastic theology to be the worst obstacle to the gospel and took it very seriously. His judgment of scholaticism also reflects the experiences of his youth. Scholasticism was the theology that had made him miserable as a friar, because it had left him to rely on his own moral abilities. But he also remained convinced about the high level of scholastic thinking. That quality was precisely what made it so dangerous, and what led him to continue the battle against it for the rest of his life.

In any fight the partners are always to some extent dependent on each other. In an intellectual fight each person has to adjust himself to his opponent. Luther did so by using one school against another, but he also returned to scholastic distinctions when they might be of help to his argument. Quite apart from the discussion about Luther's possible return to scholasticism in his contest with Erasmus, there is no question about his use of important scholastic terms and arguments. His discussion of the term *necessity,* for instance, is unthinkable without its scholastic basis. The same applies to his use of the distinction between different modes of presence in *Vom Abendmahl Christi* against Zwingli. Luther obviously felt free to return to scholastic usage whenever it could improve his arguments. This practice is quite evident in the disputations of his later years.

We can conclude that scholasticism remained a focus for Luther all his life. He continued to consider scholastic theology the most dangerous of all obstacles to the right understanding of the gospel. At the same time, he felt free to use its intellectual achievements to sharpen his wit, to defeat less competent opponents, to argue in disputations, but above all to warn against the clever ways by which men try to destroy the gospel.

NOTES

1. See the recent account by Martin Brecht, *Martin Luther: Sein Weg zur Reformation 1483–1521* (Stuttgart, 1981), 33–110.

2. For differing approaches, see Heiko A. Oberman, "Reformation: Epoche oder Episode," *Archiv für Reformationsgeschichte* 68 (1977): 56–111 and in the same volume, Leif Grane, "Lutherforschung und Geistesgeschichte: Auseinandersetzung mit Heiko A. Oberman," 302–15.

3. The basic study on Luther's notes is still Paul Vignaux, *Luther: Commentateur des Sentences (Livre I, Distinction XVII)*, (Paris, 1935).

4. This view is based on my own study of the marginal notes in *Contra Gabrielem: Luthers Auseinandersetzung mit Gabriel Biel in der Disputatio contra Scholasticam Theologiam 1517* (Gyldendal, 1962), 265–82.

5. *WA* 4:590–604; cf. *WA* 60: 333. The composition and method are both

thoroughly scholastic. The composition of the sermon on Matt. 7:12 (WA 4:590–95) is reminiscent of a *quaestio* in Gabriel Biel's *Collectorium.* First, the concepts are explained; second, the doctrine is established; and third, various counterarguments are refuted. Both the content and the manner of proof, including reason, authority, and comparison, are quite traditional. The second sermon on John 3:16 (WA 4:595–604) is also rather traditional in content. The teaching on free will, for example, is even more Ockhamist than in Luther's marginal notes. Free will is described as the most noble of all the gifts of God, without which the other gifts would be useless.

6. On the theme of Luther and tradition in the *Dictata super Psalterium,* see James S. Preus, *From Shadow to Promise: Old Testament Interpretation from Augustine to Luther* (Cambridge, Mass., 1969). The most penetrating study of Luther's sources and his way of using them in these lectures is found in a number of articles by Gerhard Ebeling, now collected in *Lutherstudien,* vol. 1 (Tübingen, 1971), 1–220.

7. Most of the passages under discussion are considered or at least mentioned in *Contra Gabrielem,* 283–309. Most recently, they have been commented on by Marilyn J. Harran, *Luther on Conversion: The Early Years* (Ithaca and London, 1983), 54–85. They also are discussed in Steven E. Ozment, *Homo Spiritualis: A Comparative Study of the Anthropology of Johannes Tauler, Jean Gerson and Martin Luther (1509–16) in the Context of Their Theological Thought* (Leiden, 1969) and in part in Michael G. Baylor, *Action and Person: Conscience in Late Scholasticism and the Young Luther* (Leiden, 1977), 119–208. References to additional literature may be found in these books.

8. See Ebeling, *Lutherstudien,* 1–220, and Reinhard Schwarz, *Fides, Spes und Caritas beim jungen Luther: Unter besonderer Berücksichtigung der mittelalterlichen Tradition* (Berlin, 1962), 76–240. Schwarz is also a reliable guide for the matters discussed above in notes 6 and 7.

9. According to WA 60:333 only three sermons belong to the period of the *Dictata super Psalterium.* They are to be found in WA 1:20–29 and 30–37 and WA 3:342–46.

10. I do not wish to overemphasize the difference between the sermons and lectures. Even the much larger body of sermons preached at the time when Luther was lecturing on Romans seems to me to be more "conservative" in form than are his lectures. My intention is to draw attention to the possibility that Luther may have found the usual manner of preaching congenial even as he was consciously trying to find new methods in his capacity as lecturer.

11. Concerning Staupitz, see David C. Steinmetz, *Luther and Staupitz: An Essay in the Intellectual Origins of the Protestant Reformation* (Durham, N.C., 1980). Steinmetz persuasively demonstrates that the attempt to find the real significance of Staupitz for Luther in *the authorship* of the Vicar General is not fruitful. This fact does not minimize the importance of Staupitz, but it does make it far more difficult to establish its exact form and content.

12. These last statements are in my opinion incontestable as long as we follow the sources. They have two important consequences: 1. the marginal notes on Peter Lombard as well as the *Dictata super Psalterium* demonstrate that it is pointless to look for anything other than a scholastic theology of an Ockhamist type as constituting Luther's background, i.e., the teaching with which he was familiar from his years as a student; 2. Luther's lack of development within the scholastic framework, even though he was changing considerably during these

years in both method and views, indicates that Luther's scholastic background could hardly have been a driving force in his progress toward a new theology. The failure to affirm these two consequences leads to pure speculation or at least to a confusion between a *condition*, namely, that Luther was originally an Ockhamist, and the *cause* of the Reformation. Conditions are certainly important in understanding an intellectual development like Luther's but they are not necessarily an explanation of that achievement.

13. WA 57:3–232. This paragraph is a very brief summary of issues with which I am concerned in the first part of my book, *Modus Loquendi Theologicus: Luthers Kampf um die Erneuerung der Theologie (1515–1518)* (Leiden, 1975). If we follow the sources, it is clear that the most essential addition to Luther's thought during this period came from his reading of the anti-Pelagian Augustine. In numerous articles and in several prefaces to books Heiko Oberman has attempted to make plausible the old theory of the influence of Gregory of Rimini as an explanation of Luther's anti-Ockhamist theology. See, for instance, "Augustin-renaissance im späten Mittelalter," part of the fascinating but somewhat confusing book entitled *Werden und Wertung der Reformation: Von Wegestreit zum Glaubenskampf* (Tübingen, 1977), 82–140. He argues his ideas most recently in the preface to *Gregor von Rimini: Werk und Wirkung bis zur Reformation*, ed. Heiko A. Oberman (Berlin and New York, 1981). For a discussion of the book, see my review in *Theologische Literaturzeitung* 108, no. 4 (1983): 275–79. On the theory of Gregory of Rimini's influence on Luther, see also David C. Steinmetz, "Luther and the Late Medieval Augustinians: Another Look," *Concordia Theological Monthly* 44 (1973): 245–60.

14. WA 1:145–51, *Quaestio de viribus et voluntate hominis sine gratia disputata*, (1516). See also Luther's letter about the disputation to Johann Lang in Erfurt, *WA Br* 1:64–69, no. 26 (middle of October 1516). A useful guide to the text material of the theses is offered by Emanuel Hirsch, "Randglossen zu Luthertexten," *Theologische Studien und Kritiken: Zeitschrift für das Gesamte Gebiet der Theologie* (1918), 108–22.

15. I have discussed Luther's efforts at greater length in *Modus Loquendi Theologicus*, 127–60.

16. Karlstadt's 151 theses of 26 April 1517 are given in Ernst Kähler, *Karlstadt und Augustin: Der Kommentar des Andreas Bodenstein von Karlstadt zu Augustins Schrift De Spiritu et Litera, Einführung und Text* (Halle, 1952), 1*–37*.

17. WA 1:224–28. See my discussion in *Contra Gabrielem*.

18. WA 59:25–53. *Eigenhändige Randbemerkungen zu Gabriel Biels Collectorium und Canonis Misse Expositio*. Seit 1516/17.

19. See Luther's letter of 9 May 1518 to Trutfetter, *WA Br* 1:170, 33–38, no. 74: ". . . ego simpliciter credo, quod impossibile sit ecclesiam reformari, nisi funditus canones, decretales, scholastica theologia, philosophia, logica, ut nunc habentur, eradicentur et alia studia instituantur; atque in ea sententia adeo procedo, ut cotidie Dominum rogem, quatenus id statim fiat, ut rursum Bibliae et S. Patrum purissima studia revocentur."

20. *WA Br* 1: 139, 27–32, no. 58 (13 February 1518): "Porro scolasticis doctoribus et canonistis constat nullam deberi a nobis fidem, dum suas opinantur opiniones. Et, ut vulgo dicitur: Turpe est Iuristam loqui sine textu. At multo turpius est Theologum loqui sine textu. Non Aristotelis dico, Nam hanc plus, valde, nimis, satis loquuntur, sed nostro, id est sacrae scripturae, Canonum, Ecclesiasticorum patrum."

21. *WA* 1:647–48, 530–31.

22. See *WA* 1:647, 30–648, 9, where Luther declared the argumentation of Silvester Prierias to be: "nuda verba . . . aut solas opiniones Divi Thomae . . .", i.e., "sine scriptura, sine patribus, sine Canonibus, denique sine ullis rationibus," 30–33, and the quotation given in n. 20.

23. Jean Rott, ed., *Correspondance de Martin Bucer*, vol. 1 (Leiden, 1979), 59–72. The specific passage I have cited is given on 61, 54–56: "Cum Erasmo illi conveniunt omnia, quin uno hoc praestare videtur, quod quae ille duntaxat insinuat, hic aperte docet et libere."

24. Bucer gives Beatus a fairly full account of the first thirteen theses and Luther's defense of them. He thereby demonstrates his understanding of the contents of Luther's "paradoxa." The interpretation I have given thus seems to be the most reasonable and likely one. How else could Bucer have perceived Luther as being in agreement with Erasmus? Bucer's description of the impression Luther made upon him confirms this view. He did not talk about Luther's doctrine, but about his manner of presentation, his ability as a disputant, and his expertise as an expositor of Scripture against the "sophists."

25. Concerning Luther's way of defending himself in the time before his meeting with Cajetan, see my *Modus Loquendi Theologicus*, 161–91, for the necessary documentation.

26. *WA Br* 1:308, 54–59, no. 136 (between 13 and 19 January 1519): "Ich fürchte auch, G.H., dass, dieweil zu unsern Zeiten die Schrift und alten Lehrer wieder herfürdringen und man nu in aller Welt anhebt zu fragen, nicht was, sondern warumb dies oder das gesagt, ob ich schon solche blosse Wort aufnähme und einen Widerruf tät, würde es nicht allein unglaubwürdig, sondern auch für einen Spott angesehen und eine öffentliche Unehre der römischen Kirchen."

27. The wide distribution of the private correspondence of Erasmus did much to confirm the impression that he was favorably inclined toward Luther—to the annoyance of the great humanist. See P. Bietenholz, "Erasme et le public allemand, 1518–1520: Examen de sa correspondance selon les critères de la publicité intentionelle ou involuntaire," in *XVIIIᵉ Colloque international de Tours: L'Humanisme allemand (1480–1540)* (Munich and Paris, 1979), 81–98. In the same volume, see Martin Greschat, "Humanistisches Selbstbewusstsein und reformatorische Theologie," 371–86, which offers an evaluation of Luther's humanist support in the first years of his public activity.

28. *WA* 6:497. Letter of dedication to *De captivitate babylonica ecclesiae*.

29. For Luther's understanding of the eucharist, and especially of transubstantiation, see *De captivitate babylonica*, *WA* 6:508–12. I discuss this question at more length in "Luthers Kritik an Thomas von Aquin in *De captivitate Babylonica*," *Zeitschrift für Kirchengeschichte* 80 (1969): 1–13.

30. I refer here to the views on Luther's later arguments with Zwingli and other reformers. The description of Luther's doctrine as consubstantiation has been very widespread. In my opinion, the concept of "substance" is inaccurate to describe Luther's understanding, but that subject constitutes a separate discussion.

3

LUTHER AND HUMANISM

Lewis W. Spitz
Stanford University

A most important aspect of the question of "Luther and Learning" is that of his own relation to Renaissance humanism and of the importance of humanism in turn for the Reformation movement. This discussion of Luther and humanism will concentrate on three major questions: 1. How much German and Italian humanism did Luther know? Which humanists did he know, and how and when did he make contact with them? 2. How extensive was Luther's knowledge of the classics and how did his knowledge compare with that of other contemporaries such as Erasmus? Did he know more than representative medieval figures did? 3. In terms of substance, what did humanism contribute to Luther's role as a reformer? The answers to these questions about Luther and humanist learning have tremendous implications for such larger issues as the relation of the Reformation to the Renaissance and the place of the Renaissance and Reformation in the periodization of history.[1]

When Luther was on his way to the Diet of Worms he rode in a wagon that was provided for him by the city council of Wittenberg. He was accompanied by a modest entourage of his personal friends and political folk associated with the Elector of Saxony. They were met at the gate of Erfurt by Crotus Rubeanus, Luther's former fellow student and friend at Erfurt who was rector at the university there. Crotus hailed Luther "as a judge of evil, to see whose features is like a divine appearance." Crotus Rubeanus, along with Ulrich von Hutten, had written *The Letters of Obscure Men*, and he was a prominent member of Mutianus Rufus's humanist circle in Gotha. Eobanus Hessus, who became the most genial poet of the evangelical movement, cried: "Rejoice, exalted Erfurt, crown thyself . . . for behold, he comes who will free you from disgrace." That Luther was regarded as a fellow humanist, particularly by the younger humanists, is well-known. In 1517 Luther was thirty-four. Most of his followers were thirty years old or younger, and many of them were young humanists. Aesticampianus, Hutten's teacher, who was over seventy, was a rare exception. Most of Luther's opponents were fifty years old or older. Erasmus was just under fifty, and Dr. Johannes Eck, a major opponent, was a bit younger, but otherwise all of his opponents were much older men. The significant thing in our context is that these young humanists hailed Luther as a leader and saw him as a part of their enterprise. Luther responded to that kind of adulation in a very interesting way that I shall discuss shortly.[2]

Humanism is a protean concept. It has appeared in Western culture in varying modalities, and the type now under discussion must therefore be defined. Is it a matter of raising once again Tertullian's time-honored but terribly shopworn question about Jerusalem and Athens in his *Prescription Against Heretics:* What has Athens to do with Jerusalem, the church with the academy, Christians with heretics? Must we renew the modern debate between Wilhelm Dilthey, the father of modern intellectual history in the form of *Geistesgeschichte,* and Ernst Troeltsch, one of the great religious sociologists, as to how the Reformation related to Renaissance culture, medieval culture, and, by implication, to modernity?

There are massive numbers of books about the concept of the Renaissance and the meaning of humanism. The humanism that concerns us and our present topic is not the humanism that implies anthropocentrism, as in the Enlightenment. It is neither the new humanism of Wilhelm von Humboldt nor the secular humanism of Corliss Lamont. Still less is it the "progressive humanism" of the Marxists. Rather, I am talking about the Renaissance humanism of Luther's day. That humanism too has been given wildly contradictory definitions, but the seismographic needle has of late been settling down to one major indicator. Paul Oskar Kristeller related the humanists to the city secretaries in Italy, to the professors of rhetoric, successors to the practitioners and teachers of the *ars dictamis* in the medieval period. Hanna Holborn Gray, now president of the University of Chicago, broadened this definition to include a special emphasis on rhetoric and argued that many non-professionals practiced it, including bishops, doctors, lawyers, and pulpiteers. The German scholar Paul Joachimsen gave humanism a more ideological definition when he described it as a "desire for the rebirth of classical antiquity, both according to form and according to norm."[3] This definition will also serve as a useful one for the present discussion, because it suggests that humanism was a matter not only of style, good Latin, but of substantive questions that have to do with classical anthropology. It is at this point where the Reformation and the Renaissance style of humanism come into the most intimate contact and reaction. As we ponder their relation, a host of problems comes immediately to mind, such as the relation of Northern humanism to Italian humanism, of humanism to scholasticism, the role of humanism in the universities, and so on. On this particular occasion we are more interested in Luther's own relation to Renaissance humanism, his role in its survival and continuity into modern times.

Luther has been depicted by some scholars as a sickly product of a decadent or aberrant form of late scholasticism. Others have declared him to be the religious proponent and theological articulator of Renaissance humanism and his teaching to be the theological expression of the Renaissance. In actual fact, Luther's struggle was an elemental religious one. His question was How can I be sure that God is gracious to me, a sinner? We must also ask another question, namely, how did Luther reach his solution? Did he attain it with or without the help of Renaissance humanism? While his scholastic theological training posed and indeed created much of the question, humanist methodology facilitated his arrival at a solution. At the same time, only the Holy Spirit through the Word offered to him the basic solution, which he so gladly embraced in his tower experience.[4] The ways in which humanism facilitated his attaining that solution constitute the most important part of this discussion.

Let us turn now to the first of the questions posed at the beginning of this essay. From November 1517 until 1519 Luther adopted the humanist name "Eleutherius," the liberated one or the liberator—a name that Luther surely did not adopt out of respect for the thirteenth pope! The Greek word for "free," which appears in 1 Cor. 9:19, "For though I am free from all men, I have made myself a slave to all, that I might win the more" (RSV), and John 8:32, "The truth will make you free" (RSV), is the same word that Luther used as his "humanist" name. During those same years Luther called the gospel *eruditio divina*, a nice humanist affectation.[5] Not only was Luther a hero to the humanists, but he consciously associated himself with their methods and preferences. For example, in the Heidelberg Disputation, April 1518, in the philosophical theses 29–40, which Luther probably did not compose himself, he expressed an Augustinian preference for Pythagoras and Plato over Aristotle.[6] He spoke of man the midpoint in a manner worthy of Pico, although he may not have adopted this manner of speaking about man from Pico, but rather from Nemesius of Emessa, the Greek Church Father. There is a great parallel between Pico's *Oration on the Dignity of Man* and Nemesius, the Church Father's, description of man.

Another example of Luther's knowledge and recognition of humanism is provided in his *Operationes in Psalmos*. At the beginning of those lectures in 1518, Luther greeted the students and then spoke of the great flowering of the arts and sciences in their time.[7] He had after all himself been the major mover in the reform of the liberal arts curriculum at the University of Wittenberg, which culminated in the changes of 1518. Luther seldom talked about the Reformation movement, but he talked often about the curricular reformation at the University. He wished to alter the mental habits of the youth, he said, so that when they came from the arts level of study to the theological faculty, their minds would not have been molded by dialectic and syllogistic thinking. Finally, in his 1519 commentary on Paul's epistle to the Galatians, he included many Ciceronian and humanist expressions.

Luther had developed this humanist interest as his negative attitude toward scholasticism and its adverse effect on theology increased. In searching for its roots in his past, some scholars have pointed to Luther's supposed experience with the Brethren of the Common Life at Magdeburg, but we know too little about his contacts with the "Nollbrüder" there to draw any definite conclusions. On the one hand, there is a widespread myth that Luther was introduced to humanism while at Erfurt University through Crotus Rubeanus, who made contact for him with the circle of Mutianus Rufus, the canon at Gotha. But that theory is not only doubtful; it is wrong, since the Gotha circle was not formed until Luther had entered the monastery in 1505. On the other hand, the University of Erfurt was second perhaps only to Heidelberg in its openness to humanistic ideas and classical influences.

From its beginnings in 1502, the University of Wittenberg had experienced the presence of humanist scholars, such as Maternus Pistoris and Nikolaus Marschalk, who gave a commencement address in beautiful Latin.[8] Although as a new and undistinguished university, obviously Wittenberg was not a leader in the field, with the advent of Melanchthon in 1518 the strong advocate of humanism had arrived. Luther had wanted Peter Mosellanus for the position, but this was an instance when his judgment was in error.[9] It was Elector Frederick the Wise who had favored choosing Melanchthon, for somewhat political reasons, but Melanchthon proved to be far superior to Mosellanus in both brilliance and learning. Luther subsequently benefited from Melanchthon's tremendous knowledge of humanism and the classics. Luther's great impact on Melanchthon is well-known—how he bullied and used him, but always loved and respected him. That is only one part of the story, however, for Melanchthon also had a continuous influence on Luther through the years. One can almost see Luther's growing interest in humanist learning.

Melanchthon's appointment was indeed fortuitous, for there was very nearly a catastrophic appointment made at the university that might have led Luther to a negative attitude toward humanism. In January 1521 Georg Spalatin recommended Justus Jonas for a professorship in Wittenberg, but the Elector offered the vacant professorship to Mutianus Rufus, the cynical canon of Gotha. Although there is considerable controversy regarding how cynical Mutianus really was, Luther was quite convinced that he was very much an Epicurean, and it would have been painful for him to have had Mutianus on the faculty. Fortunately, Mutianus turned the position down, and Justus Jonas received the offer while he was with Luther at Worms in 1521. The appointment proved to be an important one in the long run.

Leif Grane has asserted that it is much easier to distinguish humanism and scholasticism in the abstract than to differentiate a humanist from a scholastic. There is presently a new trend in scholarship that emphasizes that in the older generation there were many men who were half humanist, half mystic, or half scholastic. Luther learned some humanist attitudes from the scholastics Jodocus Trutfetter and Arnold von Usingen, whom Luther later tried to convert to the evangelical cause. While a student at Erfurt, Luther also heard Jerome Emser lecture on Reuchlin's play *Sergius,* and he read Jakob Wimpheling's *De integritate.* He also learned to love the poems of the Christian poet Baptista Mantuanus, the general of the Carmelite order who wrote in the manner of Vergil. Thus it is a mistake to interpret Luther's relation to humanism so exclusively in the light of his controversy with Erasmus. Indeed, at first Luther did not even want to respond to Erasmus, but it was Kathie who badgered him until he did so. He finally dashed off his response, *De servo arbitrio,* in a matter of weeks in 1525, the same year as he married. In short, Luther's relation to humanism was much deeper and broader than scholars have realized, and his contact with Erasmus was but one important incident in a long lifetime of study.

Luther was not vindictive toward Erasmus, for he did a translation of one of Erasmus's writings and kept some of them on his own required reading list. Indeed, some of Erasmus's works were included in the readings that the visitors were to recommend for the evangelical schools. Luther opposed Erasmus not because of his humanist learning but for theological reasons. On certain occasions Luther even imitated Erasmus. For example, in 1517 Erasmus said, "We live at the dawn of a golden era." In 1524 Luther wrote to the city councils, "We live at the dawn of the new era." His optimism reflected his awareness of the new knowledge about the natural world that was coming to light. He kept this positive spirit and great interest in the natural world to the very end, as can be seen from his *Commentary on Genesis,* which he was writing during his final years. [10]

Luther's most dramatic encounter with German humanism was clearly the incident of the Reuchlin controversy, which also demonstrated the power of the printing press. The printing press played a key role in the success of the Reformation, but even before Luther there were three periods of much printing activity, one having to do with Savonarola, one having to do with Karlstadt's debates with the Thomist scholastics, and the third having to do with the Reuchlin controversy. Luther himself wrote a famous letter to Johannes Reuchlin when he was being persecuted for defending Hebrew letters. Indeed, eventually Reuchlin was threatened and summoned to Rome. In his letter Luther sided with Reuchlin against the scholastics and wrote: "Through your power the horns of this beast have been quite badly broken. Through you the Lord brought it about that the tyranny of the sophists has learned to attack the true friends of theology with greater caution, so that Germany could again breathe after having been not only oppressed but almost destroyed for some centuries thanks to scholastic theology. The beginning of a better knowledge could be made only through a man of great gifts. For just as God trod into dust the greatest of all mountains, our Lord Christ (if one may use this analogy), and thereafter from this dust allowed so many mountains to arise, so you also would have brought forth little fruit if you had not likewise been put to death and trod into the dust, from which so many defenders of the holy scriptures have arisen."[11] Luther did not hold up Christ as an example to be followed. He is the *exemplar, non exemplum,* for He shows how God deals with humankind. Christ is thus primarily an example of that divine action, not simply of how we are to relate to God through imitating Christ.

Luther also made use of Reuchlin's scholarship, employing both his Hebrew grammar and his dictionary. Reuchlin was not particularly appreciative, but when Luther became the center of attention, he said: "Thank God, now the monks have someone who will give them more to do than I have."

Francis Bacon, in *The Advancement of Learning,* Book I, underlined the linkage between Luther and the Renaissance. "Martin Luther," he wrote, "conducted (no doubt) by an higher providence, but in discourse of reason finding what a province he had undertaken against the Bishop of Rome and the degenerate traditions of the Church, and finding his own solitude, being no ways aided by the opinions of his own time, was enforced to awake all antiquity and to call former times to his succours to make a party against the present time. . . ." The cliché of Luther's going back to the sources, *ad fontes,* like the humanists, is in all the books, and there is

indeed a positive analogy to be drawn. Does that similarity, however, make Luther a humanist? Could he have accomplished what
he did without the assistance of the most progressive intellectuals
of the time? The humanists, of course, insisted upon returning to
the sources, and this idea was so implanted in people's minds that
at least indirectly Luther was impressed by it. Nonetheless, one
cannot take this conclusion too far. For example, the mere presence of many humanists at Erfurt does not of itself establish the
linkage between Luther and humanism, any more than the presence of Italian Augustinian works in the Erfurt library proves that
Luther studied them.

Let us now turn to our second question concerning Luther's
knowledge of the classics. In short, what did Luther know about
the classics and how much of a classicist was he? On the one hand,
Luther often deprecated himself and his learning. He repeatedly
called himself a *rusticus* and frequently affirmed that his Latin was
barbarous.[12] On the other hand, there is counterevidence from
other sources. For example, Gordon Rupp analyzed the *De servo
arbitrio* and pointed out that there are many more, for its length,
classical citations in Luther's treatise than in Erasmus's *De libero
arbitrio.* Erasmus was very much a name-dropper and cited first
one and then another author, but Luther put both quotations and
ideas to genuine use. In fact, some of the editors of the Weimar
edition were sleepily unaware of the extent of classical citations
hidden in Luther's writings. To use his own analogy, they were
sometimes like the nursemaid who dozes as she rocks the cradle.
Certainly the notes on the classical citations in the *De servo arbitrio* are extremely inadequate.[13]

Luther did know the works of Lorenzo Valla, who is mostly
appreciated for his work on the elegance of the Latin language and
for his comments on free will. Indeed, Luther affirmed that Valla
and John Wycliffe were his two most important authorities. He also
kept in touch with Italian writings to a certain extent. Francesco
Pico della Mirandola, Flacius Illyricus, and other Italians spent
much time in Wittenberg. In *Culture and Anarchy,* published in
1869, the Victorian author Matthew Arnold wrote: "The Reformation has often been called a Hebraising revival, a return to the
ardour and sincereness of primitive Christianity. No one, however,
can study the development of Protestantism and of Protestant

churches without feeling that into the Reformation, too—
Hebraising child of the Renascence and offspring of its fervour,
rather than its intelligence, as it undoubtedly was,—the subtle
Hellenic leaven of the Renascence found its way, and that the exact
respective parts, in the Reformation, of Hebraism and of Hellen-
ism, are not easy to separate."[14] That was Matthew Arnold's assumption, and though he grossly overstated the case, it is true that
the Renaissance penetrated not only Luther's mind but the Reformation movement as such to a much greater extent than scholars
have realized. Protestantism itself was clearly conscious of this
inheritance and exploited it.

We can now turn to the question of Luther's knowledge of the
classics. In 1524 he wrote to the councilmen of Germany: "For-
merly no one knew why God had the languages revived, but now
for the first time we see that it was done for the sake of the gospel,
which he intended to bring to light and use in exposing and destroying the kingdom of Antichrist. To this end he gave over
Greece to the Turks in order that the Greeks, driven out and
scattered, might disseminate their language and provide an incen-
tive to the study of other languages as well."[15] That *translatio* myth
was transmitted into modern historiography largely through Theodore Beza and his history of Protestantism, but we know that
Greek learning came to the West long before the fall of Constan-
tinople. When Luther entered the University of Erfurt in 1501, he
may have come into contact with good classicists, but we cannot
prove that to be the case. For example, in a letter of 1516 to
Mutianus Rufus he wrote "our friendship is of a relatively recent
date."[16] When he came to know Mutianus well, he began calling
him a skeptic and an Epicurean. He wrote to Staupitz that he
preferred to withdraw from the scene and to observe the pageant of
brilliant people in his times. From his earliest university days on,
Luther was aware of the great intellectual developments of his
times, including both humanism and the revival of the classics.

Indeed, Luther entered the monastery with Vergil and Plautus
under his arm—a sure sign of his appreciation of the classical authors. Clearly, Luther valued both the ideas and the eloquence to
be found in the classics. He once wrote: "Were I as eloquent and
rich in words as Erasmus, in Greek as learned as Camerarius, and
in Hebrew as skilled as Forstemius, and were I younger, ah, how I

would delve into the Word of God!"[17] In 1537 he wrote on the table with chalk in Latin: "Substance and words—Philip [Melanchthon]. Words without substance—Erasmus. Substance without words— Luther. Neither substance nor words—Karlstadt."[18] Eloquence was important to Luther as a worthy expression of substantive content.

In his 1524 letter *To the Councilmen of All Cities in Germany That They Establish and Maintain Christian Schools* Luther voiced his well-known lament: "How I regret now that I did not read more poets and historians, and that no one taught me them! Instead, I was obliged to read at great cost, toil, and detriment to myself, the devil's dung, the philosophers and sophists, from which I have all I can do to purge myself."[19] If he felt the deprivation of his early years, was he able in his later years to compensate for this deficiency? The evidence suggests that he was indeed able to do so. At the Leipzig Debate, for example, Dr. Eck expressed admiration for Luther's ability in Latin, and Peter Mosellanus, who presided at the occasion, commented upon the excellence and precision of his Greek.

Four months after Luther's death Melanchthon wrote in his *Vita* that Luther had read many ancient Latin authors, including Cicero, Vergil, Livy, and others. He read them, said Melanchthon, not as youths who make excerpts but for their images of human life and for purposes of teaching, and with his firm and true memory he retained them and kept them before his eyes. Melanchthon implies that Luther did his basic reading of the classics in school and as an arts student. The texts substantiate this view, for in the *Table Talks* there are 59 references to Cicero, 50 citations from Vergil, but the historian Livy falls to one side, and there are 61 references to Aristotle. In Luther's writings and correspondence, Aristotle, Cicero, and Vergil are most frequently cited, far more than any other classical authors, followed by Terence, Horace, Plato, Quintilian, Homer, and Ovid, roughly in that order. There are individual scattered references to Aesop, Plautus, Suetonius, Herodotus, Xenophon, Ammianus, Marcellinus, Juvenal, Caesar, Aeschylus, Minucius Felix, Pliny, Tacitus, Demosthenes, Apuleius, Polycrates, Plutarch, Sulpicius, Severnus, Parmenides, Zeno, and a few others. Most of the authors whom Luther cited frequently had been published in Germany by 1520. Frequency of reference or quotation does not, of course, tell us everything, for

The German humanists, Ulrich von Hutten and Conrad Celtis, stressed the importance of the historian Tacitus. The belief that the Renaissance view of history was basically built on historical theories reflecting Livy is mistaken, for it was Tacitus who loomed large in their minds. He did so in part because he praised German virtue, but also because he described the decline of Rome. For the humanists it was very problematical to put those contradictory notions together, but it was not so for Luther. He used Tacitus to suggest the deterioration of the Germans since the pure and simple life in ancient times.[28]

Luther often included references to other classical authors in his works. He cited Pliny the Younger, for example, in his first sermon on the First Letter of Peter, of all places. Quintilian was his favorite rhetorician, as he was for most of the humanists. Luther also spoke of that distinguished man, Varro, from whom one could learn a whole array of information. He knew the geographer Pomponius Mela and used him in his commentary on Psalm 73. He termed Ovid an excellent poet, surpassing all others. According to Luther, he "masterfully expresses things in charming verse."[29] He quoted Ovid on man as the midpoint, who holds his hands upward toward the sky, hands up and eyes toward heaven, with feet planted on the ground—the only animal who can do so. In other words, Luther drew substantive things from some of the poets. He said, for example, that the enthusiasts or *Schwärmer* were like Icarus, fluttering around in the air too close to the sun. They would burn off their feathers and fall to the ground with their lofty, fluttery ideas. There are also at least twelve references in Luther's works to Horace's *De arte poetica*.

Luther also affirmed the importance of some classical authors whose works might appear to be more problematical. He advised a Silesian schoolmaster who had been criticized for having his students perform a comedy of Terence to keep on as he had done. The boys should be encouraged to put on the plays in order to practice their Latin, to develop good artistry, to see people well portrayed and reminded of their duties. Luther did not favor bowdlerizing Terence, for the obscenities show the pupils what life is really like.[30] Rather late in life Luther bought copies of Lucretius and Lucan. Of the skeptic Lucian he said that he liked such a person

the references to Aristotle, for example, are frequently pejorative. The historians proved less quotable than the philosophers and rhetoricians, which does not mean that their total impact on his thought was of less importance. In addition, it is not always possible to tell which allusions came from reading and which from conversations with friends and colleagues.

Melanchthon was the person who had a formative influence on Luther's thought about history. Luther discussed history with him, he related, even on the journey to Torgau. In later years, between 1555 and 1560, Melanchthon gave lectures on world history. A comparison of Melanchthon's *Introduction to the Chronicon* and Luther's prefaces to various historical works such as Hedio's *Chronicle* of 1539 or Cuspinian's *Caesares* of 1541 reveals many similarities in their ideas about history. Twenty years after the Leipzig Debate Luther commented that at the time he had not been well versed in history and had attacked the papacy *a priori* on the basis of Scripture, but that now he appreciated the correspondence of the histories and Scripture and could attack the papacy *a posteriori* from the histories. In 1537, in fact, Luther wrote his own sharp attack on the monstrous fraud of the Donation of Constantine. As a younger man he had been led by Hutten's edition of Lorenzo Valla's *De donatione Constantini* to conclude that the papacy was the anti-Christ.[20]

Luther developed a deeper interest in history during the final three lustra of his life. He wrote prefaces to various "historical" works: *Vorrede zu Spalatin, magnifice consolatoria exempla et sententiae ex passionibus sanctorum . . . collectae; Vorrede zu Robert Barnes, Vitae Romanorum Pontificum; Vorrede Johannes Kymäus, Ein alt christlich Konzilium . . . zu Gangro; Vorrede zu Historia Galeatii Capellae, 1539; Vorrede zu Epistola S. Hieronymi ad Evangrium de potestate, 1538; Praefatio zu Georg Major Vitae patrum, 1544; Vorrede zu Papstreue Hadrian IV. und Alexandrus III. gegen Kaiser Friedrich Barbarossa, 1545*. These prefaces show that Luther shared with the humanists a passionate interest in history. He was interested in the entire sweep of history, not merely, like the annalists and chroniclers, in particular events. His writings are replete with historical reflections and judgments.

The rising tide of cultural nationalism, which antedated the Reformation by a century and a half, increased the humanists' interest in their own people's history. Histories should not be "cold and dead," but should serve useful moral purposes. Good history requires good historians, the "lion-hearted," men not afraid to write the truth.

Luther was also fascinated with the inner meaning and nature of history. He saw God as active everywhere in history, though He is often hidden, disguised as though concealed behind a mask (*larva*). Faith sees beyond fate and chance to the God whose Word reveals the true meaning and content of history. In his introduction to Galeatius Capella's history of the reign of Francesco II Sforza, Duke of Milan, who played a key role in the relations of Charles V and Francis I, Luther declared that "histories are . . . a very precious thing," for "histories are nothing else than a demonstration, recollection, and sign of divine action and judgment, how He upholds, rules, obstructs, prospers, punishes, and honors the world, and especially men, each according to his just desert, evil or good." He added: "The historians, therefore, are the most useful people and the best teachers, so that one can never honor, praise, and thank them enough."[21]

Arnold Berger has argued that Luther saw history as a completion of the Bible and as a kind of *Weltbibel.*[22] That may be something of an overstatement, but it is true that as Luther's interest in history grew he came to see the value of chronology as an aid to exegesis and as useful for the light it sheds on church history. In 1541 he constructed his *Supputatio annorum mundi* or *Reckoning of the Years of the World,* a chronological table, so that he "could always have before his eyes and see the time and years of historical events which are described in Holy Scriptures and remind himself how many years the patriarchs, judges, kings, and princes lived and ruled or over how long a period of time one succeeded the other."[23] Possibly inspired by Eusebius, whose work he admired, he wrote three columns of events and dates for East, West, and German history and worked out parallel traditions of biblical history and secular events. He projected the dates from creation to the year 1540, dividing the table by millennia. He listed the indulgence controversy as a major event of the sixteenth century! He drew on contemporary histories to fix dates, but where there was a conflict between the scriptural data and that of some secular source, such as the chronology ascribed to Megasthenes, he opte[for the reliability of the Scriptures.

Although history was of great importance to the Wittenber[theology at the outset of the Reformation, and Luther promoted at the university, there is no real evidence that he sought to hav[chairs of history established there. In his 1520 treatise *To th[Christian Nobility of the German Nation Concerning the Reform the Christian Estate,* he did, however, declare such a step to b[desirable, but there is no evidence that he actively tried to impl[ment it.

Not only did Luther have an impressive knowledge of the cla[ics and a keen interest in history, but he also savored the use words. Like a true linguist and rhetorician he enjoyed the myste and beauty of language. Indeed, he even liked to play with wor[Much of what he wrote consisted of a mixture of Latin and G[man, what is termed a macaronic text.[24]

Luther's 1524 letter *To the Councilmen of All Cities in Germ[is the best source for his views on the classical languages. favorite classical author was Cicero, whom he valued much m[highly than he did Aristotle. He held that whoever wants to le[true philosophy should read Cicero. He also approved of Cice[moral philosophy and his speculation about proofs of the existe[of God found in his work *De natura deorum,* which Calvin utili[in the first chapters of his *Institutes.* Luther admired Cicero's [quence and once declared: "When I read Cicero's *Orations* I [so ineloquent. I feel myself stammer as a child."[25] In many resp[Cicero was Luther's model. When Luther talked about Eccles.[he said that Cicero had fully understood the meaning of vanity vexation of the spirit. Even though he shared Erasmus's adm[tion for both Cicero and Seneca, he did not go so far as did E[mus in the expression of it. For example, Erasmus said: "Wh[read pieces like that I can hardly refrain from crying out, 'O [Cicero, pray for us' or another time, 'Holy Socrates, pray for u[Luther did say that in the world to come Cicero will sit m[higher than Duke George of Saxony or Margrave Joachim [Brandenburg, who died between two whores. If they sat w[Cicero does, they would be saved![27]

Of the historians, Luther particularly liked Livy for his [

since he did not insinuate or beat around the bush. The skeptics were not like Erasmus, talking out of both sides of his mouth, but rather, they said clearly what they meant. Luther frequently used Lucian as a test of skeptical ideas.[31]

Limitations of space prevent a survey of Luther's knowledge of the Greek sources, but one must mention that Luther himself, as his personal contribution, put out an edition of Aesop's *Fables* that was used in the schools.[32]

We must now ask two questions about Luther's knowledge of the classical authors and texts. First, did he know more than any well-educated medieval figure who had completed secondary school? We must conclude that he did not know much more. He had an enormous and wonderful memory, and what he once learned he retained and continued to use. Second, did Luther, in his later years, learn even more of the classics and use them? Again, the answer must be in the negative. Certainly he did not learn a great deal more. One finds in the *Table Talks* of his later years the same style and the same references as in the early years. With more leisure he did not become a great humanistic scholar, as is sometimes said. He knew an impressive amount about the classics, much more than most educated moderns, and he was alert to Renaissance humanism and to the educational goals of the humanists. But the evangelical cause consumed his energies and prevented him from becoming an outstanding classical scholar or a giant among Renaissance humanists. Noble as were such pursuits, they were not his calling.

We may now turn to our third and final question. In terms of substance, what was the contribution of humanism to Luther's role as a theological and religious reformer? Bernd Moeller once stated with epigrammatic force: "Without humanism no Reformation." This assertion on the surface seems problematical, for Renaissance humanism did not lead to a radical Reformation in the Italy of Petrarch, Bruni, or Ficino, nor in the Spain of Cardinal Ximenes, nor in the France of Budé, Bodin, or Lefèvre d'Étaples. But in the German context humanism was clearly an essential precondition and a necessary catalyst for radical change. The Italian humanists considered scholastic theology, and some of them even Aristotelian natural science, to be a foreign import coming from the ultramontanes. The German humanists were increasingly repelled by scholasticism, admired Italian humanism, but were patriotically hostile to the Italian church and its exploitation of the German people.

The question posed here is whether Luther's reactions were the same or at least similar to those of the German humanists, and, if so, what impact humanism had upon his theology. It is clear that Luther was critical of scholastic theology, but not because the Latin was barbarous, nor merely because of the intrusion of dialectic, but preeminently because it represented a form of *theologia gloriae*. The adoption of the Aristotelian ethic reinforced the semi-Pelagian tendencies of medieval theology. Luther shared with the Christian humanists, most strongly represented in central and southern Germany, both a desire for religious enlightenment and some aspects of their cultural nationalism. His position is the same toward both mysticism with its "heavenly ladder" for ascending to the naked majesty of God and humanism with its optimistic anthropology, which did not fully grasp that sin or alienation from God is the root condition of man and that grace is a benignity whereby God by grace alone forgives man his sin and reconciles man to Himself. That difference was at the heart of the so-called free will controversy with Erasmus. The distinction has been made between humanist Christians and Christian humanism, a suggestion that is of some limited value, but that needs to be spelled out very carefully and specifically.[33] Luther has also been called a biblical humanist, a term not without its conceptual and substantive difficulties.[34] It is necessary to inquire more closely into Luther's theological and religious debt to humanism in order to place him with some precision on the spectrum of Renaissance humanism.

Such an inquiry should focus on Luther's exegesis, on his preference for rhetoric over dialectic, on the relation of moral philosophy to sanctification, on educational ideas, and finally, on the importance of the classical curriculum as a carrier of cultural and religious values.

Luther's professional calling was to teach as a *doctor in Biblia*. He was an exegete who lectured on the Scriptures as a professor for thirty-three years. In his exegesis he used the traditional sources and handbooks, such as Nicholas de Lyra's *Postillae*, extensively but not uncritically. Already in the *Dictata* or *First Lectures on the Psalms* of 1513–1515 and in his *Lectures on Romans* of 1515–1516, he made quite explicit his dependence on the French humanist Lefèvre d'Étaples, who had done annotations on the Psalms and the Pauline epistles. Lefèvre, in turn, learned much about biblical interpretation from Jean Gerson, a mystic and conciliarist whom Luther referred to as *Doctor Christianissimus.* The influence of the French evangelical humanist Lefèvre reinforced Luther's objection to the traditional fourfold interpretation of Scripture, for the al-legorical, tropological, and anagogical interpretations allowed for too much subjectivity. Even in traditional university disputations they were not accepted as proofs of the truth of an argument. Along with Lefèvre, Luther insisted upon the historico-literal interpreta-tion of the text, by which he, too, meant the spiritual message intended by the authors, holy men of God moved by the inspira-tion of the Holy Ghost. Whether this approach to exegesis, with its implied hermeneutics, was humanist in any generic or historical sense of the word may be debated, for what Luther owed to Lefèvre may have been a spiritual-evangelical approach rather than a humanist philological method. The fact that the line is hard to draw does not excuse us from making the attempt to draw it.

Another example may be of value in considering Luther as ex-egete, namely, his debt to Reuchlin, the great Hebraist. As is well-known, Luther, in contrast to supercilious Erasmus, was an ardent student and in due course a real master of Hebrew. Both his lec-tures and commentaries were mostly on books of the Old Testa-ment, which he translated with the help of his "Sanhedrin." He used Reuchlin's Hebrew vocabulary and grammar, though he con-sidered his cabalistic writings to be phantasmic and harmful. When Luther lectured on the Psalms, as the annotations in the *Dictata* make clear, he referred to Reuchlin's treatment of the seven penitential psalms. Since Luther's Hebrew was still weak in the mid-1510s, the precision of his knowledge of specific vocables and textual interpretations falls off in quality when he moves beyond Reuchlin's work.[35] Part way through his *Lectures on Romans* Luther switched to the newly published Greek New Testament text of Erasmus. Clearly Luther's dependence upon humanist philology and exegetical techniques helped him to transcend the inaccuracies, vagaries, and theological misconceptions of medieval exegesis. At the same time, for Luther the touchstone of interpre-tation remained the theological principle that an interpretation that exalts the *promissa dei et beneficia Christi* is the correct one. Any interpretation that diminishes those promises and benefits is false. It has been asserted that Luther was the first exegete since Irenaeus to enunciate so clearly a theological criterion for determining the biblical canon. He was also the first in a millennium to propose a simple religious criterion by which dark passages are to be understood in the light of a clear message. That is what Luther meant with the postulate that Scriptures are to be interpreted by the Scriptures *(Scriptura Scriptura interpretatur)*. He did not mean, as a mere humanist might, that an obscure scriptural passage must be interpreted in the light of passages that are philologically or textually more comprehensible. Though Luther's biblical exegesis derived its formal method from the rules of rhetoric, the evangelical substance came from the Scriptures by listening with the help of the Holy Spirit to the Word.

Luther owed a great debt to humanism and to certain classics for his appreciation of rhetoric over dialectic. Like Ulrich von Hutten, who had declared that knowledge that merely convinces intellectually but does not lead to action is not truth, but philosophizing in the shadows, Luther held rhetoric to be a superior form of philosophy. The Scriptures are rhetorical and are not made up of labyrinths of syllogisms. That rhetoric was an important tool for Luther and for all evangelical preachers is virtually self-evident, and the newer studies of Luther's homiletics bear this fact out nicely.[36] Moreover, Luther's emphasis upon the spoken Word of the gospel *(Verbum evangelii vocale)* suggests an affinity between rhetorical expression and the Word as the carrier of the message of salvation.

Recently the attempt has been made to establish an interior connection between the rhetorical art of moving affections or emotions *(ars movendi affectus)* and the vivification *(vivificatio)* of the sinner by the Holy Spirit. In commenting on Psalm 119:25 in the *Dictata*, "Revive me according to thy word" *(RSV)* *(Vivifica me secundum verbum tuum)*, Luther wrote: "This making alive takes place through the Spirit of God, namely, as a spiritual will. . . . No matter how learned and enlightened by faith a person may be, unless he wills and works by the same affect, he is not yet living."[37] On Psalm 119:37, "give me life in thy ways" *(RSV)*, Luther commented: "It is the Spirit who makes alive and faith which justifies, as Paul says in Romans 1:17, for the just lives by faith. 'Revive me'

(*vivifica me*) is to say 'justify me' (*iustifica me*)."[38] The conclusion
follows that Luther linked *vivificatio affectu* with *iustificatio fide*,
thus drawing upon a rhetorical locus at the very heart of his theology.[39] Again in the *Dictata*, commenting upon Psalm 119:17 (16),
"Deal bountifully with thy servant, that I may live and observe thy
word" (*RSV*), Luther wrote: "Christ's words not only have the
power to teach (*vim docendi*), but also the power to move within
(*vim excitandi seu movendi*). . . . A good speaker must know how to
do three things, to teach, to delight, and to move. Therefore, I
have never forgotten the words from the cross."[40] Christ seems to
him to be the *bonus orator.*[41] Impressive though this argument
identifying the *vivificatio ex affectu* and the *vivificatio ex fide* may
be, in the final analysis it is not convincing. For Luther, in contrast
to Petrarch and Agricola, only the Holy Spirit can turn the whole
man around from unfaith to faith and eternal life, even though
words constitute the external instrument and well-spoken words
are able to move the emotions.

In addition to their emphasis on languages and philology and
their preference for rhetoric over dialectic, the Renaissance
humanists also stressed the fundamental importance of moral philosophy. Luther had lectured on Aristotle's *Nichomachean Ethics,*
but had excoriated the Stagarite's intrusion into Christian theology.
He was an admirer of Cicero and the Roman moralists, though he
was not totally unaware of the potentially subversive nature of
Stoic moral philosophy with its nontheistic presuppositions about
natural law. Although Luther was, of course, opposed to the intrusion of moralism as a way to salvation, he appreciated the value of
moral philosophy for natural man and for the regenerate Christian
in conducting the affairs of this life. Revealed law, the Decalogue,
the Sermon on the Mount, remain the spiritual standard for Christians. The law of love is the basis for all law and should also be such
for all positive laws made by governments. Nonetheless, the experience of a statesman and moral philosopher such as Cicero can be
of tremendous value to Christian and non-Christian alike in order-
ing the matters of this world. Once again, the humanist stress on
moral philosophy finds a place in Luther's theology and has a certain utility, but it is not a source for nor a generic part of his
theology.

Finally, Luther's educational goals and ideals were conditioned

by Renaissance humanism. At no time in the history of the world,
except perhaps our own, has so much attention been paid to educational theory and reform as in the age of the Renaissance and
Reformation. The reformers were more egalitarian than the elitist
Renaissance humanists and insisted upon universal compulsory
elementary education for boys and girls. They also created the
gymnasium and Lyceé for the gifted who could benefit from secondary education in order better to serve the bureaucracies of the
state, the clerical positions of the church, and the very schools
themselves. They revised the curriculum on the university level
along humanist lines. Through the educational system, the Reformation, Protestant and Catholic, perpetuated humanist ideals, and
classical letters and values. The reformers elevated the dignity of
pedagogy by placing teaching as a divine vocation next to the
ministry of the Word.

This understanding of the educability of men did not, however,
constitute a contribution by humanism to Luther's theology as
such. In his anthropology Luther was somewhat less optimistic
than were humanist educators as to what could be accomplished
through the teaching of the *humaniora,* or liberal arts, alone. Education has a lofty place in Luther's mind, but as such it has to do
with earthly culture and human society and is not a prerequisite for
entrance into the Kingdom of God. Learning does not of itself have
salvific powers. It is the person who is enlightened by the Holy
Spirit who is made wise unto salvation. Humanist educational
theory did not contribute to the substance of Luther's theology nor
change the nature of his Christian anthropology.

In conclusion, without the contribution of Renaissance humanism Luther could not have been the effective magisterial reformer
he proved to be. He was alert to the newer intellectual currents of
his time and appreciated the achievements of contemporary
humanists. Just as he considered the Renaissance to be a John the
Baptist pointing to the coming evangelical revival, so he himself
used the new tools of humanist learning in behalf of the gospel. His
student and first biographer, Johannes Mathesius, gave the following superscription to his collection of Luther's *Table Talk* from the
winter of 1542–1543: *Evangelii occasi renascentis per doctorem.*[42]

Luther was himself a devotee of the classics, preeminently of
Latin literature, but also of Greek and Hebrew. He contributed

creatively through his own marvelous gift for languages to the development of new high German. He was appreciative of the fine arts and composed church music, hymns, and a revised liturgy. As an educator, in daily contact with the *Praeceptor Germaniae,* Philipp Melanchthon, he provided for the continuity of humanist learning into modern times—through the gymnasia, and both the new Protestant and reformed older universities. Humanism was important for Luther, and he, in turn, contributed to its ongoing presence and influence in the centuries that followed. Luther was deeply appreciative of the revival of the arts and liberal learning, the great achievements of Renaissance humanism. He wrote: "Now that God has today so graciously bestowed upon us an abundance of arts, scholars, and books, it is time to reap and gather in the best as well we can, and lay up treasure in order to preserve for the future something from these years of jubilee, and not lose this bountiful harvest."[43]

Leopold von Ranke, the great historian of the Reformation and the father of modern critical history, quite rightly paid this tribute to Luther, a man of learning as well as a great man of faith: "In no nation or age has a more . . . commanding and powerful writer appeared; and it would be difficult to find another who has so perfectly united popular and intelligent style and such downright homely good sense to so much originality, power and genius."[44]

NOTES

1. The most excellent recent study of German humanism is that of Erich Meuthen, "Charakter und Tendenzen des deutschen Humanismus," in *Säkulare Aspekte der Reformationszeit,* ed. Heinz Angermeier and Reinhard Seyboth (Munich and Vienna, 1983), 217–76, with detailed bibliographic, analytical notes. The *XVIIIe Colloque international de Tours: L'Humanisme allemand (1480–1540)* (Munich and Paris, 1979) contains a brief but significant article by Heinz Otto Burger, "Martin Luther und der Humanismus," 357–69. Otto Herding and Robert Stupperich, eds., *Die Humanisten in ihrer politischen und sozialen Umwelt: Kommission für Humanismusforschung 3* (Boppard, 1976), contains relevant essays. A handy book of sources in English translation is Reinhard P. Becker, ed., *German Humanism and Reformation* (New York, 1982). There is, of course, a vast German literature on the question of humanism and the Reformation, such as Martin Greschat and J. F. G. Goeters, eds., *Reformation und Humanismus: Robert Stupperich zum 65. Geburtstag* (Witten, 1969). I shall not, however, recapitulate the literature to which I have referred in earlier publications, for example, in the chapters, "Humanism in the Reformation," in *Renaissance*

Studies in Honor of Hans Baron, ed. Anthony Molho and John A. Tedeschi (Dekalb, Ill., 1971), 641–62, and "The Course of German Humanism," in *Itinerarium Italicum: The Profile of the Italian Renaissance in the Mirror of Its European Transformations,* ed. Heiko A. Oberman and Thomas A. Brady, Jr. (Leiden, 1975), 371–436. On the present state of research, see Dieter Wuttke, *Deutsche Germanistik und Renaissance-Forschung* (Bad Homburg, 1968).

2. On the humanists and Luther, reflecting the generation problem, see Herbert Schöffler, *Die Reformation: Einführung in eine Geistesgeschichte der deutschen Neuzeit* (Bochum, 1936), republished in his *Wirkungen der Reformation: Religionssoziologische Folgerungen für England und Deutschland* (Frankfurt a. M., 1960), 105–88; Bernd Moeller, "The German Humanists and the Beginnings of the Reformation," in *Imperial Cities and the Reformation: Three Essays,* ed. and trans. Erik Midelfort and Mark U. Edwards (Philadelphia, 1972), 19–38; and Lewis W. Spitz, "The Third Generation of German Renaissance Humanists," in *Aspects of the Renaissance: A Symposium,* ed. Archibald R. Lewis (Austin and London, 1967), 105–21, reprinted in *The Reformation: Basic Interpretations,* ed. Lewis W. Spitz, 2d ed. (Lexington, Mass., 1972), 44–59.

3. Paul Joachimsen, "Der Humanismus und die Entwicklung des deutschen Geistes," *Deutsche Vierteljahrsschrift für Literaturwissenschaft und Geistesgeschichte* 8 (1930): 419–20.

4. See Marilyn J. Harran, *Luther on Conversion: the Early Years* (Ithaca and London, 1983), "Luther's Tower Experience," 174–88.

5. On Luther's adoption of the name Eleutherius, see Bernd Moeller and Karl Stackmann, *Luder-Luther-Eleutherius: Erwägungen zu Luthers Namen, Nachrichten der Akademie der Wissenschaften in Göttingen I. Philologisch-Historische Klasse,* no. 7 (1981), 171–203.

6. WA 1:355, 16–19; *Luther's Works,* vol. 31: *Career of the Reformer: I,* ed. Harold J. Grimm (Philadelphia, 1957), 41–42. Theses 36 and 37 read: "Aristotle wrongly finds fault with and derides the ideas of Plato, which actually are better than his own. The mathematical order of material things is ingeniously maintained by Pythagoras, but more ingenious is the interaction of ideas maintained by Plato." 42. See also Karl-Heinz zur Mühlen, "Luthers Kritik am scholastischen Aristotelismus in der 25. These der 'Heidelberger Disputation' von 1518," *Lutherjahrbuch* 48 (1981): 54–79; and Helmar Junghans, "Die probationes zu den philosophischen Thesen der Heidelberger Disputation Luthers im Jahre 1518," *Lutherjahrbuch* 46 (1979): 10–59.

7. WA 5:19, 16–20; 20, 19–25; 26, 6–14. For Luther's role in university reform at Wittenberg, see Max Steinmetz, "Die Universität Wittenberg und der Humanismus (1502–1521)," 103–39, and Kurt Aland, "Die Theologische Fakultät Wittenberg und ihre Stellung im Gesamtzusammenhang der Leucorea während des 16. Jahrhunderts," 155–237, in *450 Jahre Martin-Luther-Universität Halle-Wittenberg,* vol. 1: *Wittenberg 1502–1817* (Halle, 1952). See also Martin Brecht, *Martin Luther: Sein Weg zur Reformation 1483–1521* (Stuttgart, 1981), "Universitäts-und Wissenschaftsreform im Bund mit dem Humanismus," 264–84.

8. *Nicolai Marscalci Thurii oratio habita albiori academia in alemania iam nuperrima ad promotionem primorum baccalauriorum numero quattuor et viginti anno domini mcccciii,* trans. with introduction and notes by Edgar C. Reinke and Gottfried G. Krodel (St. Louis, 1967), printed for Valparaiso University.

9. On Melanchthon's humanism, see Adolf Sperl, *Melanchthon zwischen*

Humanismus und Reformation: Eine Untersuchung über den Wandel des Traditionsverständnisses bei Melanchthon und die damit zusammenhängenden Grundfragen seiner Theologie (Munich, 1959); Wilhelm Maurer, *Der junge Melanchthon zwischen Humanismus und Reformation*, vol. 1: *Der Humanist*, vol. 2: *Der Theologe* (Göttingen, 1967 and 1969), and Walter Elliger, ed., *Philipp Melanchthon: Forschungsberichte zur vierhundertsten Wiederkehr seines Todestages dargeboten in Wittenberg 1960* (Göttingen, 1961). On Mosellanus, see Oswald Gottlob Schmidt, *Petrus Mosellanus: Ein Beitrag zur Geschichte des Humanismus in Sachsen* (Leipzig, 1867).

10. WA 42:4–56; *Luther's Works*, vol. 1: *Lectures on Genesis. Chapters 1–5*, ed. Jaroslav Pelikan (St. Louis, 1958), 3–73 on Genesis 1.

11. Johannes Reuchlin, *Johann Reuchlins Briefwechsel*, ed. Ludwig Geiger (Stuttgart, 1875), 311, no. 227, Luther to Reuchlin, 14 December 1518. Ludwig Geiger, *Johann Reuchlin: Sein Leben und seine Werke* (1871; reprint, Nieuwkoop, 1964), 353ff., discusses the relation of Luther and Reuchlin.

12. E. Gordon Rupp and Philip S. Watson, eds., *Luther and Erasmus: Free Will and Salvation*, vol. 17 in *The Library of Christian Classics* (Philadelphia, 1969). Luther, in the *De servo arbitrio*, wrote: "Yet not only do I not blame them, but of myself I yield you a palm such as I have never yielded to anyone before; for I confess not only that you are far superior to me in powers of eloquence and native genius (which we all must admit, all the more as I am an uncultivated fellow who has always moved in uncultivated circles), but that you have quite damped my spirit and eagerness, and left me exhausted before I could strike a blow." 101–2.

13. WA 18:600–787.

14. Matthew Arnold, *Culture and Anarchy*, ed. William S. Knickerbocker (1869; New York, 1929), 139.

15. WA 15:37, 11–26; *Luther's Works*, vol. 45: *The Christian in Society II*, ed. Walther I. Brandt (Philadelphia, 1962), *To the Councilmen of All Cities in Germany That They Establish and Maintain Christian Schools* (1524), 359.

16. WA Br 1:40, 7–8, no. 14 (29 May 1516). On 2 May 1515 Johann Lang had brought to Mutian a copy of Luther's sermon of 1 May along with Luther's greetings. On Luther's lack of contact with Mutian prior to that time, see Hans von Schubert, "Reformation und Humanismus," *Lutherjahrbuch* 8 (1926): 7.

17. WA TR 1:487, 21–23, no. 961.

18. WA TR 3:460, 38–40, no. 3619. *Luther's Works*, vol. 54: *Table Talk*, ed. and trans. Theodore G. Tappert (Philadelphia, 1967), 245.

19. WA 15:46, 18–21; LW 45:370.

20. Brecht, *Martin Luther*, 329–30. WA Br 2:48, 30–49, 29, no. 257 (24 February 1520).

21. WA 50:383, 8; 384:2–5, 15–17. *Luther's Works*, vol. 34: *Career of the Reformer IV*, ed. Lewis W. Spitz (Philadelphia, 1960), 275–76.

22. Arnold Berger, *Martin Luther in kulturgeschichtlicher Darstellung* (1895; Berlin, 1919), 553.

23. WA 53:22–184; 22, 13–18. Ernst Schäfer wrote the pioneering work *Luther als Kirchenhistoriker: Ein Beitrag zur Geschichte der Wissenschaft* (Gütersloh, 1897). See also Karl Bauer, *Die Wittenberger Universitätstheologie und die Anfänge der Deutschen Reformation* (Tübingen, 1928), "Die Bereicherung der Wittenberger Theologie durch die Geschichte," 80–98. Werner Elert, *Morphologie des Luthertums hauptsächlich im 16. und 17. Jahrhundert*, vol. 1 (1931; Munich,

1958), 426, n. 2, discusses the question of whether Luther and then Melanchthon wished to establish chairs for historians, which would have been an advance over Italian universities. Three works on Luther's understanding of history especially worthy of mention are John M. Headley, *Luther's View of Church History* (New Haven, 1963); Heinz Zahrnt, *Luther Deutet Geschichte: Erfolg und Misserfolg im Licht des Evangeliums* (Munich, 1952); and Hans-Walter Krumwiede, *Glaube und Geschichte in der Theologie Luthers: Zur Entstehung des geschichtlichen Denkens in Deutschland* (Göttingen, 1952). On the importance of Luther and the Reformation for the history of universities, see the recent volume by Leif Grane, ed., *University and Reformation: Lectures from the University of Copenhagen Symposium* (Leiden, 1981).

24. Birgit Stolt, *Die Sprachmischung in Luthers Tischreden: Studien zum Problem der Zweisprachigkeit* (Stockholm, 1964), 8–15. See also the outstanding though still unpublished dissertation of Sandra Mosher Anderson, *Words and Word in Theological Perspective: Martin Luther's Views on Literature and Figurative Speech* (Ph.D. diss., Northwestern University, 1973). On Luther's genius for language, see also Heinz Bluhm, *Martin Luther: Creative Translator* (St. Louis, 1965).

25. Cited in Oswald Gottlob Schmidt, *Luther's Bekanntschaft mit den alten Classikern: Ein Beitrag zur Lutherforschung* (Leipzig, 1883), 14. The *Table Talk* is replete with comments on the excellence of Cicero on the subjects of proofs of the existence of God, the immortality of the soul, the rhetorical impact of the orator, the blessedness of life, and annihilation after death. One of the telling passages in which Luther draws a line between revelation and Cicero's natural wisdom occurs in *WA TR* 3:4, 19–24, no. 2808b; *LW* 54:171: "Experience demonstrates the efficacy of divine truth. The more it's read, the more it works. With all his wisdom and eloquence Cicero couldn't achieve this, although he was supreme in human wisdom. Such wisdom can't rise above its own level but must remain under it. Cicero was the wisest man. He wrote more than all the philosophers and also read all the books of the Greeks. I marvel at this man who, amid such great labors, read and wrote so much."

26. In Erasmus's colloquy *The Religious Banquet,* following a conversation about the wisdom of Cicero, Cato, and Plato, Erasmus has Nephalius declare: "Indeed, it was a wonderful elevation of the mind in a man who did not know Christ nor the Holy Scriptures and therefore I can scarce forbear, when I read such things of such men but cry out, *Sancte Socrates, ora pro nobis.*" For a discussion of the problem, see Lewis W. Spitz, *The Religious Renaissance of the German Humanists* (Cambridge, Mass., 1963), 197–236; 212.

27. *WA TR* 5:311, 7–9, no. 5671; *LW* 54:475. Luther said that he hoped God would look with favor upon Cicero even though he was a pagan. *WA TR* 4:14, 1–4, no. 3925.

28. Frank L. Borchardt, *German Antiquity in Renaissance Myth* (Baltimore, 1971), 104–9. See also Hajo Holborn, *Ulrich von Hutten and the German Reformation,* trans. Roland H. Bainton (New Haven, 1937), 44–45; 55; 76–77; Lewis W. Spitz, *Conrad Celtis: The German Arch-Humanist* (Cambridge, Mass., 1957), 93–105.

29. Schmidt, *Luther's Bekanntschaft mit den alten Classikern,* 31.

30. *WA TR* 1:430–31, no. 867. See Schmidt, *Luther's Bekanntschaft mit den alten Classikern,* 23, 25. E. G. Sihler, "Luther and the Classics," in *Four Hundred*

Years: Commemorative Essays on the Reformation of Dr. Martin Luther and Its Blessed Results (St. Louis, 1916), 252.

31. Sihler, "Luther and the Classics," 253; Schmidt, *Luther's Bekanntschaft mit den alten Classikern*, 58.

32. *WA Br* 5:309, 13–15, no. 1563 (8 May 1530): "I have also proposed to prepare the fables of Aesop for the youth and the common crowd so that they may be of some use to the Germans." See Lewis W. Spitz, "Headwaters of the Reformation: *Studia Humanitatis, Luther Senior, et Initia Reformationis*," in *Luther and the Dawn of the Modern Era: Papers for the Fourth International Congress for Luther Research*, ed. Heiko A. Oberman (Leiden, 1974), 107.

33. Josef Ijsewijn, "The Coming of Humanism to the Low Countries," in *Itinerarium Italicum*, 282.

34. The term *biblical humanism* is, for example, used by E. G. Schwiebert, *Luther and His Times: The Reformation From a New Perspective* (St. Louis, 1950), "Triumph of Biblical Humanism in the University of Wittenberg," 275–302; and J. Lindeboom, *Het Bijbelsch Humanisme in Nederland* (Leiden, 1913).

35. Werner Schwarz, "Studies in Luther's Atittudes Toward Humanism," *Journal of Theological Studies* 6 (1953): 66–76. See also Hans Volz, "Luthers Arbeit am lateinischen Psalter," *Archiv für Reformationsgeschichte* 48 (1957): 44ff., 53; and Walter Koenig, "Luther as a Student of Hebrew," *Concordia Theological Monthly* 24 (1953): 845–53.

36. The latest excellent study of Luther's homiletics relates his sermonic method to rhetorical principles such as the *inventio, genus deliberativum, genus demonstrativum* and *iudicale*, and so forth, Ulrich Nembach, *Predigt des Evangeliums: Luther als Prediger, Pädagoge und Rhetor* (Neukirchen-Vluyn, 1972), 117–74. He relates Luther's sermons to Quintilian's teaching on counselling the people, 139–72, a point spelled out by Eric Wittenborn, *Luthers Predigt vom Jüngsten Tag (Theologische Darstellung, homiletische Form, grundsätzliche Bedeutung)* (Bonn, 1964), and Hermann Werdermann, *Luthers Wittenberger Gemeinde wiederhergestellt aus seinen Predigten: Zugleich ein Beitrag zu Luthers Homiletik und zur Gemeindepredigt der Gegenwart* (Gütersloh, 1929). Luther made immediate application to local problems when preaching in the City Church, where he had become a kind of assistant pastor shortly after his permanent return to Wittenberg, but much more formally and generally when preaching away from Wittenberg. He was always textual, with only about seventy of his some three thousand extant sermons not based specifically on a sermon text. See also Martin Doerne, "Luther und die Predigt," *Luther: Mitteilungen der Luthergesellschaft* 22 (1940): 36–77.

37. *WA* 4:320, 37–39.

38. *WA* 4:325, 8–9.

39. This argument is made by Heinz Otto Burger, "Martin Luther und der Humanismus," 364–67.

40. *WA* 4:284, 32–33, 36–285, 1.

41. Burger, "Martin Luther und der Humanismus," 366–67.

42. Ibid., 364.

43. *WA* 15:52, 25–29; *LW* 45:377. See Ernst Lichtenstein, "Luther und die Humanität," *Evangelische Theologie* 10 (1951): 393. Luther, nevertheless, gave precedence to the influence of the *Spiritus Sanctus* over human *ingenium*, to stammering religious truth over smooth human eloquence, and to Christian faith

over antique learning. See the excellent article by Helmar Junghans, "Der Einfluss des Humanismus auf Luthers Entwicklung bis 1518," *Lutherjahrbuch* 37 (1970): 37–101.

44. Leopold von Ranke, *Deutsche Geschichte im Zeitalter der Reformation*, vol. 2, 6th ed. (Leipzig, 1881), 56.

4
LUTHER THE EDUCATIONAL REFORMER

James M. Kittelson
The Ohio State University

"Little Wittenberg," Luther is reported to have called it. Little it was indeed, as well as new. In addition, Luther himself was apparently not much to talk about as he began his career as a professor there. In 1513 one Paul Lange took a tour of German universities to interview, for a book he was writing, both those who were already famous for their learning and those who, so rumor had it, would likely become learned and famous. It may be something of a surprise that he included Wittenberg in his itinerary. It is certainly at least a curiosity that in doing so he did not interview Martin Luther.[1]

Nonetheless, Luther's Reformation and in particular his reform of education were already under way, even though he himself was doubtless not aware of it. In the first place, as the voluminous research into his early lectures shows, Luther's thought on the critical questions of justification, righteousness, faith, and grace was already in motion. He was thus maturing as a professor and beginning to revise the things that he had been taught as a student. In addition, he was already acquiring skills in the humanistic disciplines that would lead by 1518 and thereafter to a thorough reform of the curriculum at his own university and thence to many others.[2] Finally, the Reformation itself may be rightly understood as a massive educational undertaking that in time affected entire

95

populaces. People, and in particular, ordinary people, had to be taught the new religion.[3] Consequently, in spite of what might be first impressions, the subject, "Luther the Educational Reformer," is by no means just one more slice of the reformer's career. It is an issue that lies at the very heart of understanding Luther, the Reformation, and at least one dilemma within modern Christianity.

If only by way of underlining the point, it should be added that this assertion is by no means an invention of scholarly hindsight. Luther himself knew that education was a critical issue. In 1518, on his way back from the Heidelberg Disputation where for the first time he put before a large and learned audience the basic outlines of his theology, he wrote one of his colleagues the following lines: "I sincerely believe that it is impossible for the church to be reformed unless the canon law, the decretals, scholastic theology and philosophy, and logic, as they now exist, are absolutely eradicated and other studies substituted."[4] Two years later he went to a larger public on the issue in the famous treatise *To the Christian Nobility of the German Nation Concerning the Reform of the Christian Estate*, where he declared: "The universities, too, need a good and thorough reformation. I must say that, no matter whom it annoys."[5] Then in 1524 he published a treatise *To the Councilmen of All Cities in Germany That They Establish and Maintain Christian Schools*, in which he argued with typical vigor that all cities should found schools for their children. "Even though only a single boy could thereby be trained to become a real Christian," he declared, "we ought properly to give a hundred gulden to this cause for every gulden we give to fight the Turk, even if he were breathing down our necks."[6] Six more years passed, and he returned to the subject of education again, this time with a sermon in which he urged all the temporal authorities to force children to attend school.[7] Finally, in one of his last acts, just a few days before his death, Luther participated in the founding of a Latin school in Eisleben, and in so doing included detailed instructions with respect to who was to pay the bills of the new school.[8] Certainly, he was a great theologian, a pastor, and a biblical scholar, but from the beginning of his career to its end, he was also an educational reformer, who not only spoke his mind but also acted on his convictions.

Three difficult problems nonetheless confront those who would embark upon an investigation into Luther and education. In the first place, the term *education* is a very slippery one. "What is being taught?"; "How is it being taught?"; and "What is the desired outcome?" are just three of the many questions that need clear answers. In the second place, for all his interest in the subject, Luther was not the primary creator of curricular changes during the sixteenth century and especially not at the lower levels. For the most part, this work was left to individuals like his colleague Philipp Melanchthon, who was much more securely grounded than he in the educational program of Renaissance humanism.[9] Finally, and to complicate matters much more, education at all levels was the subject of intense debate just before and during the early years of the Reformation. Before we proceed with the discussion, therefore, it is very important to clear away an enormous underbrush of possibly misleading preconceptions.

Proceeding with these issues in reverse order focuses attention first on the Renaissance debate over education. Briefly, the humanists' critique of contemporary learning and education centered on one charge, namely, that propositional knowledge as taught by the schoolmen bore no fruit in daily life and therefore detracted from the proper educational enterprise. Thus, for logic or dialectic, the intellectual cornerstone of scholasticism, they would substitute rhetoric, grammar, and the ancient languages. In religion, the search for doctrinal truth was to be replaced by poetry and history to the end of gaining enlightened piety. If Aristotle, the father of them who know, was not to be removed entirely from the curriculum, then only his *Rhetoric* and *Poetics* were to be read. For the humanists, true knowledge was not universal and propositional in character but concrete and specific to time and place. Its fruits were not *scientia* or knowledge but *sapientia* or wisdom, which was to be found in the marketplace and in the conduct of daily life rather than in the lecture hall or the monastery. Education thus had an end both temporally and finally. This end was the finished person who came out of the classroom and into society, and who, in the words of Leonardo Bruni, was studying without appearing to be studious.[10] The good man was thus not the possessor of many doctrines in some specialized field of learning, but the one who could apply general principles in a variety of specific situations.

To illustrate, this emphasis upon general classical learning was most evident in the humanists' universal preference for moral philosophy over philosophy strictly conceived. It took form in their abhorrence of the disputation, the most common late medieval method of acquiring and disseminating knowledge. One by-product of this inclination, and a very important one in this context, was a powerful interest in the particular "spirit" of a text, rather than whatever universal truths might be drawn from it. One example, drawn from the study of law, must suffice to demonstrate the point. It is the idea of ἐπιείκεια or equity in enforcing the law and the corresponding notion of *summa ius summa iniuria* or "the full force of the law produces the greatest injustice."[11] Simply put, the idea is that individual cases must be adjudicated according to the spirit or intent of the law rather than according to its letter. Thus, any law that might be expressed abstractly abruptly loses its universal character at least in the sense that it no longer applies to specific cases in anything like the way a cookie cutter may be applied to cookie dough. Circumstances must always be taken into account. For the humanists, the endless academic debates in search of pure justice were thus irrelevant exercises in futility, and the truth of general doctrines was, if not unknowable, then certainly irrelevant to the vital business of the conduct of life.

The intellectual proclivities of the Renaissance are very much to the point here precisely because Luther was a recipient of this humanist educational critique.[12] Indeed, in many respects he and the movement that flowed from him did the one thing that the Renaissance humanists could never accomplish. He institutionalized their educational ideals in both the lower schools and the universities, and he did so in three ways.

First, Luther personally was at the forefront of a movement to reform his own university. By 1523 all the proposals that he had spelled out in private correspondence in 1518 and in the treatise *To the Christian Nobility* of 1520 were in place. Aristotle's dialectic, the disputations, and canon law were removed from the curriculum and their place taken by rhetoric, grammar, the ancient languages, and, above all, the Bible.[13] These reforms then spread to other universities, both old and new, in Lutheran lands—Tübingen, Marburg, and Strasbourg, for example. As already indicated, Luther aided in the founding of primary schools, such as the Latin school at Eisleben, which also embodied the latest educational thinking of figures such as Erasmus.

Second, the reform movement provided the crucially important financial resources to accomplish these goals on a scale never dreamed of before. Many European cities could, to be sure, boast of municipal schools but they were usually founded by means of essentially private funding and were haphazardly supported at best. In brief, the reformers now persuaded the secular authorities to take the income that had supported convents, monasteries, and the like and to turn it into resources for schools. Ecclesiastical prebends thus became the sixteenth-century equivalent of endowed chairs for teachers and professors, and the movement to establish public schools was underway. [14]

Finally, as already noted, Luther provided leadership for the educational movement as he did in so many other areas. In the treatise *To the Christian Nobility* of 1520 he clearly endorsed the humanist educational program. Interestingly, the 1524 letter *To the Councilmen* in which he urged the establishment of schools was substantially repeated in an appeal by Strasbourg's reformers to their magistrates in August of the same year, and then reiterated at some length in the preface to a Hebrew grammar published by one of their number in 1525. [15] Again, Luther was the pacesetter.

At this point, however, a problem arose for the reformers and therefore for all students of the subject. To explain requires a closer look at Luther's educational writings and also comes full circle to the first question, the one concerning the nature of education. On the one hand, Luther certainly was a recipient of the humanist educational program. On the other hand, he was also a late medieval professor as well as an evangelical reformer for whom the learning and teaching of true doctrine were essential. Surely, this is the meaning of his thunderous reply to Erasmus, "*Spiritus sanctus non skepticus est!*"—the Holy Spirit is not a skeptic—at the beginning of *De servo arbitrio*. [16] In sum, the problem is that both the Renaissance ideal of the enlightened Christian citizen and the Reformation ideal of teaching true doctrine coexisted in the minds of Luther and others. As has already been pointed out, there are some respects in which these ideals conflicted with one another.

Yet they were both present in Luther's principal educational writings from the very first. In the address *To the Christian Nobility*, for example, he criticized the place of Aristotle in the curriculum, not because it led to "barbarism," the humanists' favorite epithet, but because it both detracted from the gospel and was contrary to it. Additionally, when he declared that the Bible should be the core of the theological curriculum, he did so on the assumption that the Scriptures are clear and simple and that they point to Christ alone. He most definitely did not intend that students should steep themselves in the Bible simply for the purpose of acquiring biblical knowledge that was doctrinally free. Rather, they were to find there the Word of God, that is, the sound doctrine upon which Luther's reform movement was based from the very first.

As the years passed, he in fact distinguished between the two purposes of education ever more sharply—to the benefit of its role in the teaching of true doctrine. A comparison of his two works on basic education is instructive. In the first, the letter *To the Councilmen,* he declared that proper schooling would be of benefit to both the church and society at large. He insisted: "If . . . there were no need at all of schools and languages for the sake of the Scriptures and of God, this one consideration alone would be sufficient to justify the establishment everywhere of the very best schools for both boys and girls, namely, that in order to maintain its temporal estate outwardly the world must have good and capable men and women. . . . "[17] By comparison, Luther began the second work, *A Sermon on Keeping Children in School,* with a lengthy discussion of the need for trained pastors, and then added to it arguments for the wisdom of teaching those who would in time become leaders of the body politic. But, when faced with the obligation to demonstrate why those who would take up neither calling should be educated, he turned to a rather different argument from what he had used before. No longer did he set forth the general need for a trained citizenry; now he declared that "other boys as well ought to study, even those of lesser ability . . . for we need not only highly learned doctors and masters of Holy Scripture but also ordinary pastors who will teach the gospel and the catechism to the young and ignorant, and baptize and administer the sacrament."[18] Those who were so educated, but did not become pastors (even "ordinary pastors") in the normal course of events would form a "ready reserve" in case of emergency. Almost apologetically, he added that such an education would not harm anyone's ability to earn a living and would positively help the management of a household.[19]

The difference between these two works, the one written in 1524 and the other in 1530, reflects more than a slight shift in emphasis from an author who normally paid scant attention to strict consistency. Rather, it corresponds to a real shift in Luther's own concerns, from developing and disseminating his understanding of the gospel to ensuring its survival. It is common practice among historians to attribute this change to Luther's reactions to the Peasants' War, the appearance of the radicals, and the Sacramentarian Controversy, and therefore to date it around 1525.[20] It is more likely, however, that Luther set his mind to this new task as a result of a direct and very rude awakening both he and his colleagues experienced between 1527 and 1529.

The source of this shock was the visitation of parishes that Lutheran princes, notably Elector John of Saxony, undertook beginning in 1527.[21] In the midst of one of the most difficult periods of his life, Luther himself followed their preparation, conduct, and results with keen interest. He personally approved the visitation articles, defended them against their critics, and encouraged the visitors in their work. "What miseries we see here!", he exclaimed after learning the early results.[22] Then, in early January 1529, after personally serving as a visitor, he wrote Elector John: "we maintain, believe, and know that Your Electoral Grace can have ordered no better work than the visitation."[23] Later the same month, he wrote Martin Görlitz, a pastor in Braunschweig, "Just now I am turning to the preparation of a catechism for the ignorant pagans."[24] What Luther saw in the visitation reports was not just that priests had left their parishes, that donors to the work of the church had reclaimed their property, or even that German peasants were a crowd of drunken louts with the sexual mores of a herd of rabbits. What Luther saw was religious ignorance, and he determined to do something about it.

Given the context of the Renaissance debate over education and its preference for the generally enlightened citizen over the learned *doctor*, there is a certain irony in Dr. Luther's decision to treat in part the situation he faced by writing catechisms. As noted, he genuinely adhered to the humanists' educational program. At the same time, the catechisms were his sole direct contribution to the curriculum of the primary schools, and they consist of doctrine at the most accessible level. Next to the Bible or portions thereof, his *Small Catechism* was in fact used in the schools to teach sound doctrine and the ability to read at the same time. Thus, while Erasmus collected his *Adages* and sayings from the ancient authors so that students might acquire both piety and good Latin while copying them, Luther did the same with his catechisms; but for piety he substituted true doctrine, and for Latin the vernacular.

At this juncture a question very naturally poses itself. Did this conflict between wisdom and doctrine that existed in principle exist also in fact? Or is it another instance of the historian's ability to overrationalize the past? In this case the tension between the educational objectives of the Renaissance and those of the Reformation was real, so real that it produced public wrangling on at least two occasions, once at Basel in the 1530s and later at Strasbourg in the 1570s.

In Basel the issue took the form of two struggles between church and university, first over how much educational attainment should be expected of pastors and second over whether the university should control the church or the other way around.[25] The person of interest is one Wolfgang Capito, the Strasbourg reformer whose Hebrew grammar was referred to earlier, and a person who had strong ties to Basel. With regard to the first issue he squarely backed education for pastors of a humanistic kind, declaring: "What harm is it to a pastor that he is a member of the society of the learned and the learning? We absolutely require everything that we have been taught; why should it be a shame that I have learned in school those things that God has given to others by spiritual understanding?" But he added that the granting of degrees in theology, that is, the training of pastors, and "the governance of the churches should be bound togther and should not be torn apart from one another. . . ." If they were divided, he argued, "the university will become heathen and stand in eternal enmity to the churches, with unquestionable evil consequences for the churches."[26] Theology or religious knowledge was thus not just a matter of learning, and it could not be left simply to the universities.

The issue between these two educational ideals came to an even more sharply focused controversy in Strasbourg itself a generation later. It did so, at least in part because this city, on the advice of its reformers, decided to establish precisely the sort of educational programs Luther advocated. On the one hand, it imported Johannes Sturm, who became perhaps Europe's most famous educator of the period, to develop and become lifetime rector of a humanist academy that exists to this day. On the other hand, the reformers themselves had very early begun giving theological lectures, in addition to preaching and their other activities, for the purpose of providing pastors for both the city's urban and rural parishes. This practice grew into both a quasi-faculty of theology at the Academy and two "Preachers' Colleges" that, through their financial and intellectual resources, were soon educating pastors for much of southwestern Germany along the Rhine River. The source of the potential problem was that students destined for the ministry followed both the theological lectures given by those pastors who were also professors and the regular curriculum of the Academy. Overlapping purposes for education thus created overlapping institutions. In the 1570s the question was, who had authority over these students' lives and studies? Was it to be Sturm, the Rector of the Academy, or Johann Marbach, a professor of theology and the president of the Company of Pastors?[27]

Ever since the nineteenth century, scholars have regarded this controversy in solely personalistic and institutional terms.[28] But the real issue that lay between the two men was the divergent educational objectives of the Renaissance and the Reformation. Sturm started the fight in December 1569 when he charged Marbach and the Preachers' Colleges with obstructing the work of the Academy and then requested a vote of confidence from its lay board of supervisors. When such was not immediately forthcoming, he offered his resignation.[29]

The ensuing struggle lasted five years and was replete with both personal abuse and charges of doctrinal impurity—standard fare for the sixteenth century. Very quickly, nonetheless, the two parties came down to basics. On the one side, Sturm's target was the Preachers' Colleges. Indeed, the heart of his reform proposal was that they should be subject to the Academic Assembly, "for it is from these two colleges that barbarism insinuates itself into our school."[30] The plan of study that he proposed for the Preachers' Colleges was in fact so weighted toward the typical humanistic curriculum that it included catechetical instruction only in the eighth and ninth classes. In just this regard, Sturm's reasoning as to why the professors at the Academy should be admitted also to voting membership in the Company of Pastors is most revealing. "For we other professors," he charged, "are excluded and cast out of their theologians' assembly and are considered by them to be such unlearned people, who know nothing about the business, and so inept and incomprehending that we do not understand such matters and cannot judge and consider them. . . ."[31]

Here was the standard humanist complaint, complete with charges of "barbarism," against academic theologians. For Marbach, by comparison, it was unthinkable for nontheologians, however learned, to have any authority over theologians. In all universities, he declared, the faculty of theology judged its own affairs just as other faculties judged theirs.

When the controversy erupted again in 1580, the same issue was at stake. This time the occasion was pressure from the theologians and the Company of Pastors for the city to adopt the Formula of Concord complete with the so-called *condemnamus* section in which subscribers condemned all who held opposing views. "What will transpire after the Formula of Concord is subscribed to. . . ?", Sturm questioned. He asked: "Will not the same be forthcoming as so unfortunately occurred at Heidelberg, Jena, Leipzig, and Wittenberg," where opponents were subsequently driven from their posts?[32] A Tübingen theologian, one Lucas Osiander, who entered the fray put the opposite side's point of view just as clearly. He said that Sturm was perfectly qualified to study the orations of Cicero, Demosthenes, and Quintilian, and to explain the writing of Homer, but in seeking also to judge true doctrine, he was exceeding his grasp with his reach. "To explicate religious controversies reliably and to interpret sacred letters does not belong to all people," he declared. This was the work of professionals.[33]

There was thus a genuine, albeit usually latent, conflict between the humanists' pursuit of wisdom and the reformers' drive to pure doctrine, however much they may have agreed about what constituted proper preparatory studies. And yet, for the most part, the two continued to coexist in Luther's universities. As a result, German high culture became overwhelmingly humanistic even in the midst of the doctrinal wars that forged Lutheran Orthodoxy during the second half of the sixteenth century.[34] But there is something far more important than all these preliminaries. This alliance between humanism and evangelical religion, however uneasy at times, was extraordinarily productive. From it came the fundamentally modern notion, one peculiar to Protestantism, that true religion even at the most popular levels is something that can be known as well as felt and acted upon.

It is true that from Christianity's very beginnings there has been something of a tension between religion of the head and religion of the heart. But generally, as with Origen or Augustine, for example, it was thought that this was a distinction of importance only to intellectuals. Origen, for one, explicitly distinguished between the religion that was sufficient for the simple and the mysteries that were available to the learned. Augustine's own pilgrimage of the soul was a profoundly intellectual one that concluded in the famous dictum, *credo ut intelligam*, I believe so that I may know. It may even be argued that the exhortation so common to the late Middle Ages, to "do what is within you," was a theological prescription for action based upon feelings, and one that was formulated by the learned for the simple. In sum, the idea that religion could be a matter of knowledge was reserved to the learned.

Luther and the Reformation changed this situation drastically. Naturally enough, it did so first with the clergy. One of the most common complaints about the pre-Reformation parish priest was that he was an ignorant lout, little different from the rude peasants he served. The most recent research suggests that there was in fact some truth to the complaint. By the end of the sixteenth century a very different situation prevailed. In the territory of Sponheim, for example, the proportion of university educated clergy rose from 22.5% in 1560 to 78.1% in 1619. In Zweibrücken the figures are 33.3% and 92%. Later the figures continued to rise. In the Palatinate the proportions increased between 1590 and 1619 from 85.9% to 94.3%. These figures are especially impressive when one notes that in addition the number of pastors rose from 99 to 423. As might be expected, given its strong schools, Strasbourg also illustrates the change. During a twenty-three-year period at the end of the century, a total of 132 persons were nominated for parish posts. Of these, 97 or 73.5% were Masters of Arts—no "ordinary pastors" these! It is true, as one scholar recently put it, that Lutheran pastors became "intellectuals. . . close to the people."[35]

Moreover, these pastors conducted their ministries in many respects as an educational program even if local schools were unavailable, as they were in many rural areas. The catechisms have already been mentioned, and it must be added that catechetical instruction remained one of the pastors' first tasks, at least if they wished to remain pastors for very long. By the end of the century, when the superintendent or the president of the local Company of Pastors came to town for the annual visitation, he commonly concluded his business by ringing the church bell, calling all the children together, and grilling them on the catechism. With surprising frequency, they could in fact recite it.[36]

It was not merely education in general that was sought by these pastors and their superiors. The main point was and remained true doctrine, as the role of the catechisms well indicates. There are also indications that other leaders of the church took Luther's doctrinal concerns equally seriously and in other ways. One verse of a common canticle sung in the Palatinate at the end of the century makes the point clearly. It is dedicated to the pastors: "God give us grace and strength that we may earnestly teach the faith, ward off false teachings and life, and further God's word and work."[37] Another example of doctrine at the parish level is a hymn written by Paul Speratus, who died in 1551. The first stanzas summarize Luther's teachings with remarkable fidelity: "Salvation unto us has come by God's free grace and favor; good works cannot avert our doom; they help and save us never. Faith looks to Jesus Christ alone, who did for all the world atone; He is our mediator. Theirs was a false, misleading dream who thought God's law was given that sinners might themselves redeem and by their works gain heaven. The law is but a mirror bright to bring the inbred sin to light that lurks within our nature."[38] This is pure Luther, even to his understanding of the Christocentric character of the law!

All of this emphasis upon the doctrinal orientation of Luther and his clergy is by no means to argue that their humanistic education disappeared in the lives and careers of clerical and lay leaders of the church. The two continued to coexist just as they did throughout the educational system. To illustrate, at the end of the century one pastor wrote a few lines about himself that may well have applied to most Lutheran pastors. He asserted: "I have learned strict logic thoroughly and read the thick books of rhetoric. I have become acquainted with the spheres of the heavens, with what physics does for me, what ethics brings forth from morals, and even to count out the rhythm of Homer."[39] This pastor was a veritable Faust, with the exception that he knew very clearly what constituted the truth.

Thus, humanism remained, conjoined to the Reformation, just as it had been in Luther's own mind. It must be added, however, that the humanist educational ideal endured in a manner that no Petrarch, Erasmus, or Sturm would have approved. It remained as a method, as can be seen clearly in the manner these pastors, and their parishoners, were taught the new faith. The great irony is that, without the humanist educational methods, without the languages, history, and rhetoric, and without the *loci* method in particular, the very emphasis upon doctrine that so characterized the Reformation at the most popular levels would be inconceivable.

Just how these doctrinal concerns moved from the university lecture hall, the disputations and the exchanges between scholars to the common person requires explanation. In the first place, it should be emphasized that Luther never thought that the doctrinal fruits of the evangelical religion should be left to the learned. In 1519, for example, he published a *German Explanation of the Lord's Prayer for the Simple Laity,* in which may be found his entire doctrine of law and gospel.[40] Indeed, so many of his early works were published in the vernacular, and therefore presumably intended for the laity, that the group of humanists in Basel felt it necessary in 1518 to translate them into Latin for the learned but non-German reading public! Nonetheless, as argued above, the great change occurred as a result of the visitations of 1527–1529 and following. Suddenly it became apparent to Luther and his colleagues that preaching at the Castle Church in Wittenberg or lecturing at the University would not accomplish the reform. The next step was the publication of catechisms that served as summaries of evangelical doctrine for the laity. As *A Sermon on Keeping Children in School* of 1530 well attests, it was also necessary to create a new clergy, if only to guarantee a supply of "ordinary pastors who will teach the gospel and the catechism to the young and ignorant. . . ."[41] Luther's seriousness about this undertaking is evident not only from his 1530 *Sermon* but also from the fact that his own correspondence during this period is filled with reference letters for placing one or another student in a particular post and letters of encouragement for those already placed.[42] Finally, he and his colleagues employed the methods of the humanists to train this new clergy. One of these methods in particular curiously reinforced the tendency to equate true religion with true doctrine.

To explain how this irony should come to pass requires a brief excursion into the history of hermeneutics and exegesis. It is well-known that for Luther the Scriptures were authoritative because they contain Christ and Him crucified in both the Old Testament and the New. In the Old Testament, Luther found not so much concrete predictions of Christ's coming (although he found these too) as a dramatic foreshadowing of God's gracious work with his people. For Luther the work of salvation was then completed in the New Testament in the life, death, and resurrection of Christ. Both the law and the gospel thus had their focus in Christ, with the law as preparation and the gospel as fulfillment. Since Christ was the central point of view of the authors of the Scriptures, Christ is the canon of the Scriptures and therefore the content of all proper exegesis. Consequently, for Luther the Scriptures became the *verbum pro me* or the living saving Word that was preached. The authority of the Scriptures derives from their content, which is Christ, and does not exist apart from Christ.

Specific doctrines flowed from this fundamental belief. Given the situation in which they found themselves as a result of the visitations, Luther and his colleagues were faced with a problem. How were they to communicate the evangelical understanding of the gospel to as many candidates for the ministry as possible, as accurately as possible, and as quickly as possible? Here was where Melanchthon, with Luther's hearty concurrence, entered the picture. He decided to employ what has been called the *loci* or *topoi* method. The *loci* or *topoi* method is borrowed from classical rhetoric. According to it, for purposes of communication, any subject—be it astronomy, medicine, law, or theology—has within it certain topics or commonplaces that are specific to it and that must be discussed if a treatise or lecture on the subject is to be successful. These are, so to speak, the issues essential to the subject under discussion. Thus in 1521 Melanchthon published his *Loci communes* or *Common Places of Evangelical Theology* in an attempt to communicate Luther's evangelical religion efficiently and accurately.[43] Many others of most religious persuasions used the same method throughout the century.

The *Loci communes* were books of Christian doctrine in the same way the catechisms were, albeit for a more learned audience. They were not, however, intended for the classroom but rather as introductions to biblical study. After all, Luther had laid down quite clearly, and Melanchthon concurred, that books other than the Bible, even those "of all the holy fathers should be read only for a time so that through them we may be led into the Scriptures."[44] Therefore, in the classroom, evangelical theology must be communicated through scriptural exegesis.

The *loci* method was employed once again. Through an interesting syllogism one can easily see why it should be so. All proper treatment of any subject considered the commonplaces of the subject. The Scriptures are authoritative in all matters essential to salvation. Therefore, they must speak clearly to all the topics or commonplaces of evangelical theology. Consequently, as a method of teaching, the professor was obligated to lay out for his students what each book of the Bible pronounces with respect to each of the basic evangelical doctrines. Certainly the exegete would employ the ancient languages, history, and grammar to understand and communicate the vitality of the text, but it was equally certain that the text spoke clearly to the principal theological concerns of the time.

One example will illustrate the results of this educational method. It comes from Marbach, the president of the Company of Pastors in Strasbourg, who became embroiled with Sturm and the Academy. He had been a student at Wittenberg in the 1540s, and Luther himself had chaired his doctoral disputation. The text is notes from his lectures on John, given between 9 August 1546 and 21 January 1547, not long after he left Wittenberg and during a period in which he may be counted upon to have taught more or less as he had been taught. At Strasbourg, Marbach used the *loci* method to explain the Gospel of John and in so doing both turned it into a treatise on predestination and argued precisely the doctrine of election that both Luther and, in particular, Melanchthon taught. Although he treated the idea several times during his exposition, one anamoly is most revealing of what this particular text became in his hands. He bluntly introduced the subject at the story of the healing of the official's son toward the end of John 4, with the explanation that Jesus "is teaching us about the will that once was hidden," that is, that Christ came to save all.[45] However, a discussion of predestination might more appropriately have occurred at John 3:18, "He who believes in him is not condemned; he who does not believe is condemned already. . . ." (RSV). Perhaps Marbach did not want to discuss election there because it would have forced him to emphasize predestination or what he and the Lutheran confessions called God's "hidden will." In any event, it is clear that he was not giving a series of lectures on John but on the doctrinal contents of John—a procedure he had learned at the University of Wittenberg.

Through adopting this basically humanistic educational method, Melanchthon and many other loyal followers of Luther thus introduced a subtle shift in the evangelical understanding of the contents of the Scriptures. No longer did they contain just Christ and Him crucified or the verbum pro me; they also contained all the doctrines that were necessary for salvation. The Bible became a book of doctrines. In this way, the reformers' use of humanistic educational goals and of the loci method in particular powerfully encouraged the tendency to equate true religion with true doctrine, even at the most popular levels.

A certain intellectualization of religion naturally followed. But, it must be asked, is this another of the many cases in which the purposes of the great leader were subverted by his lesser followers? Did Luther really believe that true doctrine equalled true religion regardless of the inclinations of the heart or the nature of public behavior? Luther was much too much the pastor for such an absurdity. Yet the matter is more complicated than quick answers might suggest, as Luther's description of the ideal pastor makes clear: "First, a good preacher should be able to teach well, correctly, and in an orderly fashion; secondly, he should have a good head on his shoulders; thirdly, he should be eloquent; fourthly, he should have a good voice; fifthly, he should have a good memory; sixthly, he should know when to stop; seventhly, he should be constant and diligent about his affairs; eighthly, he should invest body and life, possessions and honor in it; ninthly, he should be willing to let everyone vex and hack away at him."[46] There are nine items on this list, and the first six are intellectual rather than moral or affective virtues. In addition, he began his list with the ability "to teach well, correctly, and in an orderly fashion." Such teaching occurred both in preaching and in catechetical instruction, as *A Sermon on Keeping Children in School* well attests.

There can be no doubt, then, that Luther the educational reformer contributed to the modern world not only by insisting that basic education be available to all—and by making it so—but also by bringing to common people the fundamental notion that true religion could be a matter of the mind as well as of the heart and public behavior. From the training of pastors, to the catechisms, to the hymns, Luther's educational reforms in fact did much to create the modern world, with its typical distinction at the popular level between religion of the head and religion of the heart.

There has already been one irony in this story, the irony that the humanists, with their aversion to general propositions and to a religion of doctrine, should have provided the principal methods by which the reformers could create a religion of doctrines and establish an educational system that brought this creation to the common people. This irony is on Erasmus. It is only fitting that Luther should suffer the same fate. For Luther, ever the late-medieval professor, did not distinguish between the religion of the heart, and the religion of the mind. In the preface to his *Large Catechism* he declared: "I must still read and study the Catechism daily, yet I cannot master it as I wish, but must remain a child and pupil of the Catechism, and I do it gladly." Surely these are strange words to come from the book's very author! But Luther thought that in this act something spiritual was taking place. "In such reading, conversation, and meditation," he added, "the Holy Spirit is present and bestows ever new and greater light and fervor, so that day by day we relish and appreciate the Catechism more greatly."[47] As his doctrine of the "whole man" surely implies, for Luther the head and the heart were one.

It was the Enlightenment and, in particular, for the Anglo-American tradition, John Locke, who divided the heart from the mind. For Luther and the humanists, although in different ways, each prompted the other. But it was Luther, above all, who brought education to the public. It was he who argued that the average person could in some sense know what he believed, and who acted upon this conviction. Without this work, contemporary Christians would be facing very different difficulties from those confronting them now. The need to make religion make sense, and to do so for the average person, would not exist.

NOTES

1. E. G. Schwiebert, *Luther and His Times: The Reformation From a New Perspective* (St. Louis, 1950), 293ff.

2. For the most recent studies, see Michael G. Baylor, *Action and Person: Conscience in Late Scholasticism and the Young Luther* (Leiden, 1977), and Marilyn J. Harran, *Luther on Conversion: The Early Years* (Ithaca and London, 1983), and the literature cited there. Schwiebert, *Luther and His Times*, 293ff.

3. Gerald Strauss, *Luther's House of Learning: Indoctrination of the Young in the German Reformation* (Baltimore, 1978), is correct on this point, however much his general conclusions may be faulted. On a related matter see Karl Bauer, *Die Wittenberger Universitätstheologie und die Anfänge der Deutschen Reformation* (Tübingen, 1928).

4. *WA Br* 1:170, 33–36.

5. *WA* 6:457, 28–29; *Luther's Works*, vol. 44: *The Christian in Society I*, ed. James Atkinson (Philadelphia, 1966), 200.

6. *WA* 15:30, 4–7; *Luther's Works*, vol. 45: *The Christian in Society II*, ed. Walther I. Brandt (Philadelphia, 1962), 350.

7. *WA* 30/2:517–88; *Luther's Works*, vol. 46: *The Christian in Society III*, ed. Robert C. Schultz (Philadelphia, 1967), 213–58.

8. *WA Br* 12:370–71, no. 4300 (16 February 1546).

9. Karl Hartfelder, *Melanchthon als Praeceptor Germaniae* (Berlin, 1889), and Georg Karl Mertz, *Das Schulwesen der deutschen Reformationszeit im 16. Jahrhundert* (Heidelberg, 1902).

10. The literature on Renaissance educational ideals is enormous. For standard interpretations, see Paul Oskar Kristeller, *Renaissance Thought: The Classic, Scholastic, and Humanist Strains* (New York, 1961), 3–23; William J. Bouwsma, *Venice and the Defense of Republican Liberty* (Berkeley, 1968), 1–11; and James D. Tracy, *Erasmus: The Growth of a Mind* (Geneva, 1972), esp. 131–32.

11. Among his many works on the subject, see Guido Kisch, *Erasmus und die Jurisprudenz seiner Zeit* (Basel, 1960).

12. See, for example, where Luther went out of his way to defend studying the ancient languages, *WA* 15:35–37; *LW* 45:357–58.

13. Schwiebert, *Luther and His Times*, 293ff.

14. See James M. Kittelson, "Humanism and the Reformation in Germany," *Central European History* 11 (1976):303–22.

15. James M. Kittelson, *Wolfgang Capito from Humanist to Reformer* (Leiden, 1975), 211ff. The text is *Institvtionvm Hebraicarum Libri Duo V. Fabritio Capitone Autore* (Argentorati, 1525), sig. aiii-av$^{9(v)}$.

16. *WA* 18:605, 32; *Luther's Works*, vol. 33: *Career of the Reformer III*, ed. Philip S. Watson (Philadelphia, 1972), 24.

17. *WA* 15:44, 24–29; *LW* 45:368.

18. *WA* 30/2:545, 8–11; 546, 1–2; *LW* 46:231.

19. *WA* 30/2:546, 10–11; *LW* 46:231.

20. See Mark U. Edwards, Jr., *Luther's Last Battles: Politics and Polemics, 1531–46* (Ithaca, 1983), esp. 1–19 for a discussion of the problem of the "old Luther."

21. On the visitations, use with care Strauss, *Luther's House of Learning,* esp. 249–67. See also James M. Kittelson, "Successes and Failures in the German Reformation: The Report from Strasbourg," *Archiv für Reformationsgeschichte* 73 (1982):153–74.

22. *WA Br* 4:603, 11, no. 1350 (8 November 1528).

23. *WA Br* 5:3, 20–22, no. 1371 (9 January 1529). See also, for example, *WA Br* 4:230–32, 234, 241, 244, esp. 603–5.

24. *WA Br* 5:5, 22, no. 1372 (15 January 1529). For an earlier comment to Spalatin, see *WA Br* 4:624, 8–11, no. 1365 (middle December 1528?): "Ceterum miserrima est ubique facies Ecclesiarum, Rusticis nihil discentibus, nihil scientibus, nihil orantibus, nihil agentibus, nisi quod libertate abutuntur, nec confitentes, nec communicantes, ac si religione in totum liberi facti sint."

25. The controversy is treated in some detail in Kittelson, *Wolfgang Capito From Humanist to Reformer,* 214–17. The central text is Ein disputation vom Doctorat. D. Wolfgang Capitons. M.C. xxxv. Darum dise frag erwegen und gehandelt wirdt. Ob in der Gemein Gottes möge der name oder titel eines Doctors sein. Archives municipales de Strasbourg. Varia Ecclesiastica, 18:329–43[v].

26. Ibid., fol. 330[v].

27. The most recent work on the Academy is Anton Schindling, *Humanistische Hochschule und Freie Reichsstadt: Gymnasium und Akademie in Strassburg, 1538–1621* (Wiesbaden, 1977).

28. See, for example, Charles Schmidt, *La Vie et les travaux de Jean Sturm* (Strasbourg, 1855), esp. 171–205.

29. In general, see Schindling, *Humanistische Hochschule,* esp. 113ff.

30. Archives municipales de Strasbourg, Archivum St. Thomae 327:fol. 124[v]–25.

31. Marcel Fournier and Charles Engel, eds., *Les Statuts et privilèges des universités françaises depuis leur fondation jusqu'en 1789, 4/1 Gymnase, Academie, Université de Strasbourg* (Paris, 1894 = Aalen, 1970), 181–82; 174–79; 165.

32. Ibid., 188, 218.

33. Ibid. *Lvcae Osiandri Theologiae Doctoris Antisturmius vnus* (Tübingen, 1579), 31–32.

34. See, for example, Lewis W. Spitz, "The Importance of the Reformation for Universities: Culture and Confession in the Critical Years," in *Rebirth, Reform, and Resilience: Universities in Transition, 1300–1700,* ed. James M. Kittelson and Pamela J. Transue (Columbus, Ohio, 1984), 42–67.

35. Bernard Vogler, *Le Clergé protestant rhenan au siècle de la réforme (1555–1619)* (Paris, 1976), 75–76, 365. For Strasbourg, Archives municipales de Strasbourg, Archivum S. Thomae 74: fol. 3–47.

36. Kittelson, "Successes and Failures in the German Reformation," 163–65, but see also Strauss, *Luther's House of Learning,* 222–23.

37. Vogler, *Le Clergé protestant rhenan,* 365.

38. Ibid.; *Lutheran Book of Worship* (Minneapolis and Philadelphia, 1978), #297.

39. Vogler, *Le Clergé protestant rhenan*, 55, n. 17.

40. *WA* 2:80–130.

41. *WA* 30/2:546, 1–2; *LW* 46:231.

42. On Luther's students, see Lewis W. Spitz, "Luther's Social Concern for Students," in *The Social History of the Reformation*, ed. Lawrence P. Buck and Jonathan W. Zophy (Columbus, Ohio, 1972), 249–70.

43. For general developments, see Walter J. Ong, S.J., *Ramus: Method and the Decay of Dialogue* (Cambridge, Mass., 1958), esp. 92–167.

44. *WA* 6:461, 4–5; *LW* 44:205.

45. Universitätsbibliothek Tübingen. Commentaria Eiusdem D.D. Ioan. Marbachij in Euangelistam Joannum. Mc 181, fol. 51. On Marbach, see James M. Kittelson, "Marbach vs. Zanchi: The Resolution of Controversy in Late Reformation Strasbourg," *The Sixteenth Century Journal* 9 (1974): 31–44, and the literature cited there.

46. Cited in Hermann Werdermann, *Der Evangelische Pfarrer in Geschichte und Gegenwart* (Leipzig, 1923), 17.

47. Theodore G. Tappert, ed. and trans., *The Book of Concord: The Confessions of the Evangelical Lutheran Church* (Philadelphia, 1959), 359.

5

LUTHER'S CHALLENGE TO ROMAN CATHOLICISM

Daniel Olivier
Catholic University of Paris

As the variety of contributions in this volume demonstrates, the topic "Luther and Learning" can be approached from many perspectives. I wish to approach it in the light of what today's Catholics experience as they read the writings of Martin Luther.

Catholics have never read much of Luther's works. In the sixteenth century, convinced readers of Luther became Protestants. Those who remained faithful to the Roman tradition assumed that they knew enough about Protestant heresies without reading what Luther had actually written. The papal bull *Exsurge Domine* was merely concerned with Luther's errors, and this proved representative for centuries of Catholic Luther reading. Luther's writings were placed on the *Index*, books Catholics were not permitted to read.

This situation has changed only recently with the new wave of Catholic Luther research, which developed in the wake of Joseph Lortz, author of the seminal book *Die Reformation in Deutschland*.[1] Catholic scholars have come to accept Lortz's idea that Luther was, after all, also a Catholic, not simply a heretic. With this so-called Catholic Luther, the way is now open for an unprecedented Catholic experience with Luther's writings and teachings. It is now possible to read our fellow Catholic so that we may learn from him. However, many contemporary Catholic readers of

115

Luther at the academic level have become primarily interested in scholarly studies and discussions. It has been my privilege, perhaps my calling, to read Luther simply for the joy of reading his works, as one reads one's favorite author. Reading Luther has also become basic for all of my teaching at the Catholic University of Paris, where most of my students are Roman Catholics. My personal and scholarly experience in Luther reading gives me a vantage point from which to survey how contemporary Catholics react to Luther's influence.

In this paper I wish to tell of some of my discoveries with regard to both the topics "Luther and Learning" and "Luther and Catholicism." Today's Catholic reaction to Luther's writings demonstrates that his teachings challenged Catholicism also as a cultural factor, along with criticizing the papal system and Roman doctrine. The challenge becomes particularly significant today in the context of modern discussions about Western rationality. The culture of the Western world originates in the Christian Middle Ages, and many problems that arise for us on the issue of reason, or science, have already been considered by Luther in his contest with the Roman Church. An examination of this cultural challenge of Luther's permits a number of conclusions as to what may really be Luther's lasting contribution to learning.

Twenty-five years ago, under the guidance of my teacher Joseph Lortz, at the Institute for European History in Mainz, West Germany, I began reading Luther's works. At the time I was a young Catholic priest, with an advanced level of knowledge in Catholic theology but with virtually no knowledge of Luther and even less acquaintance with Protestantism. I had been taught only Luther's heresies, and the Catholic refutation of them. It had been demonstrated to me that the Christian truth was entirely on our side— knowledge nearly every Catholic obtained without ever opening one book of Luther's. The naive premise of my initial reading of Luther, then, was simply to inquire on which precise grounds he had been condemned.

Lortz's guidance helped me to become familiar with the "Catholic" Luther. The objection has been raised that Lortz's historical approach was primarily concerned with what was consonant in Luther's teaching with modern Catholic orthodoxy, so that what is perceived as "Catholic" in Luther does not really contribute to a better understanding of Catholicism. Following after Lortz, the next generation of the new Catholic Luther scholarship has gone several steps farther. For example, Otto Hermann Pesch has successfully moved the discussion to the matter of Luther's *reformative* thought, as a "possibility" for present Catholic theology.[2]

In the course of time I have become convinced that in his writings Luther deals primarily with his own Catholicism, in order to decipher what is genuinely Catholic and what is not. His talent in this endeavor is, in my opinion, unsurpassed. Rather than "father in the faith," as Peter Manns suggests, I would call Luther an expert, indeed, *the* expert on what Catholicism really is, and/or should be.[3]

In my own career in Luther studies, I decided that my task should be to teach people to read Luther the proper way, as a means of attaining clarification of their own Christian faith. I have been engaged in this enterprise now for many years, and it has been the great surprise of my life to see, year after year, that Luther's teaching on the Christian faith exercises a powerful and positive attraction to contemporary Catholic minds. This reaction seems to me to offer a clue about what really happened during the Reformation period. Whatever the numerous factors were that accounted for the phenomenon of the Reformation, it is clear that the primary factor was Luther's appeal to Catholic consciences in the matter of *faith*.

In acquainting Catholic students with Luther's texts my method is to overlook the controversial issues, at least in the first run. These issues, theological, historical, and so on, belong to the concerns of past generations, which have produced thousands of books about them, books anyone interested is free to read. Many are no longer vital, especially after the Second Vatican Council and the beginning of the ecumenical dialogue between Rome and the Protestants in 1965. Today's Catholics are actually becoming able to read Luther without focusing on his heresies, to read him in an unprejudiced way. In that respect they are similar to many people in the sixteenth century who loved what Luther published, without necessarily approving of everything he wrote. Luther had a unique talent to raise and consider the most fundamental questions, whatever one thinks of his solutions.

In a two-week period I can introduce a new group of students to reading Luther. The experiment is based on lengthy passages of ten or twelve pages—not on short quotations. It results in a constant discovery—a two-sided reaction to Luther. On the one hand, we recognize that Luther's faith is our faith; on the other hand, what Luther convinces us of cannot be our faith on today's Catholic terms.

What Luther believes is clearly what we Catholics believe. Hardly a student of mine escapes reading Luther's texts without having undergone a process of achievement in his own faith. I might add that this method of reading Luther proves as productive with Protestant, and even with Greek or Russian Orthodox students, as with Catholics. However, the more a Catholic comes to appreciate Luther, the more it becomes obvious that his conception of Christianity does not fit into our Catholic framework of thought and life.

For example, in Luther's treatise *The Freedom of a Christian*, 1520, faith is not merely a theological virtue. The Christian is subject to no one, and obviously not to the pope. Only the Word of God makes a Christian, and Luther's concept of the ministry focuses on preaching the Word of God. Faith has little to do with dogma. According to this treatise, the common priesthood of believers is the only priesthood that develops from Christ's priestly office. Good works are of no avail for salvation. On the whole, one must rely on the Bible, not on papal pronouncements.

Even more than the dogmatic difficulties, what disturbs us most today is this challenge to our Catholic basic structure of life and thought. We are used to elaborating on the Christian faith in ontological categories, which Luther, along with the Bible, ignores, and Christian existence in Catholicism is regulated by quite a number of practical observances, while for Luther faith itself is more than enough. Thus, as Catholics, we cannot live and think the way that Luther clearly and convincingly indicates—or perhaps only privately, as a number of Catholics seem to have done in the sixteenth century.[4]

Until the present time it seemed that the obstacles Luther presented to Catholics were his condemned heresies, or his behavior, his unusual hostility toward the pope, his marriage to a nun, and other such facts. But the experience I am telling shows that even when the old controversies no longer prevent Catholics from involving themselves with Luther's faith, they are simply unable to assimilate what they like in him and can recognize as also their own faith.

Luther's challenge to the Catholic framework as such becomes clearly visible in the context of contemporary Catholic experience with the *Reformator's* writings. This cultural challenge was undoubtedly also at the root of many a difficulty in Reformation times. I need not justify my opinion that Catholicism has remained basically the same since Luther nor the assumption that between Luther and Rome there has been more than doctrinal or disciplinary conflicts. Luther contested openly the importance of good works toward salvation but even more the very Roman Catholic *framework* itself, the rational pattern imposed upon the understanding of the gospel in the Church of the Middle Ages. In the last analysis, his view of Christianity was really different from that of Catholicism, but not in the first place on account of purely theological differences.

The Roman Church could already have learned from Luther in the sixteenth century to question the rational presuppositions of her dogma. But Catholicism has never learned very much from Luther. The other papers in this volume demonstrate that Luther's contribution to learning must be considered on a broader level than that of its intellectual impact within the Roman Church. One can certainly mention facts that show Luther's cultural influence on Catholicism, but it was the Jesuits or the Spanish theological school that initiated new methods of thought in sixteenth-century Catholicism.

As I became aware of the precise way in which Luther's view of Christianity was still calling my own Catholic faith into question, I did not know how to deal with the issue. There was little to read on this aspect of the conflict between Luther and Catholicism. On the whole, doctrinal discussions about Luther revolve around classical theological questions without inquiring into the conflict itself between two incompatible views of Christianity, two different cultural perspectives. Such books as the recent study by Karl-Heinz zur Mühlen on the "reformative" critique of reason and modern thought prove helpful, but they discuss the matter from the viewpoint of Protestantism.[5] It is finally the contemporary research on reason, thought, and language, the crisis of philosophy and of our

Western culture, that has opened my mind to the significance of Luther's challenge, and, in addition, to its import for the issue of learning.

There is much to be said about Luther's relationship with modern thought. After five hundred years or so the time has come to realize that the *Reformator* tried to influence in a decisive way the evolution toward the so-called New Age—and that he failed. Recent developments in the contemporary critique of modernity, such as Theodor W. Adorno's negative dialectic, tend to show that Luther was right in his appreciation of cultural problems that had taken shape throughout the development of the medieval Church and did but steadily increase after him, until our generation started to grow restless anew about them.

The subject that I shall term Luther's negative dialectic is a huge field of research, a new land that opens up to us. I consider it my personal contribution to Luther's quincentennial and to this symposium at Wittenberg University, Ohio, to reopen the road that started from Wittenberg University, Saxony, in the sixteenth century—a road that has been blocked by the Roman Catholic condemnation of Luther and by the conversion of Protestantism to what Luther most fiercely opposed, humanism, that is, justification through *reason* alone.[6]

In the following discussion I shall but put my finger on the map, without tracing out the promises of this new land. I hope, however, to convince the reader that in the years to come Luther research will be in a position to cope with the problems that plague most particularly the modern mind: God and evil. These prospects are to a great extent substantiated by the new Roman Catholic understanding of Luther, as I shall demonstrate.

My discussion begins with the critique of reason, which we now see that Luther shares with many thinkers of the present. As a theology student, I had been made aware of Luther's forceful opposition to human reason. In the Catholic framework of thought and life, reason (nature) is basic in every respect. Traditional Catholic reaction to Luther on this issue has always been to suspect, accuse, and reject Luther's undifferentiated anti-rationalism, his quietism or laxism, and to do so on theological terms. Luther's attacks upon reason were deemed to proceed from a heretical interpretation of Scripture and tradition.

As I became interested in the rapidly developing controversies that constitute the contemporary spiritual and cultural crisis of the Western world, I was struck by the great number of authors who specialize in even more destructive attacks upon reason than the ones Catholic orthodoxy reproves in Luther's works.[7] From every corner, be it philosophical, scientific, psychological, or linguistic, the rational convictions, the absolute confidence and faith in human reason that the Enlightenment seemed to have established once and for all against any dogmatic or religious authority are under fire. Indeed, modern Catholicism is suffering far worse on this account now than it did on account of Luther. Today's Catholics are often anxious to recover the gospel at the cost of the rational framework still strongly imposed by Rome. They do not become Protestants, but many merely stop listening to their Church's teachings and no longer comply with Roman decrees. In most cases they do so without ever having read one line of Martin Luther.

There is more to this situation, however, than the simple fact that Luther was not so wrong when he saw in reason the whore that prostitutes itself to all the idols of human history. What modern thought has come only recently to find objectionable and problematical with reason and its solutions is already—cloaked in medieval and theological attire—to be found in Luther's controversies with the Roman orthodoxy. It is possible to show this by borrowing from a few contemporary theologians who have given attention to the problems of reason and of theological dialectic, what also decisively characterizes Luther's thought. These scholars include such diverse people as the Reformed and Barthian Thomas F. Torrance, the Lutheran Gerhard Ebeling, and the Jesuit Jared Wicks.

Torrance is particularly interested in the theory of theology, which he regards as a science that can be compared with any other science. His book *Theological Science* is an impressive discussion of the issue of theological epistemology.[8] In a more recent work entitled *Theology in Reconciliation* he investigates the function of theology "in relation to the dualistic structures of thought and life which informed Graeco-Roman culture, science, and religion."[9] An aim of his is to reexamine the difficulties to which such structures gave rise in the formulation of the Church's understanding of the gospel.

What strikes me most about Torrance's approach is the idea that

Christian theology, and the dualistic structures of thought and life of our Graeco-Roman culture, science, and religion must and do actually conflict. Torrance indeed affirms that the structures inherited from Graeco-Roman civilization have remained the foundations of thought and life up to our times. Thus the gospel conflicts with the Church's understanding of the gospel because the Church espouses the frameworks of thought of succeeding cultural periods.

Later on in his book, Torrance advocates a reconciliation between the Christian churches on the basis of a nondualistic scientific culture that has been developing since Einstein's cosmological concepts began to replace the old Ptolemaic-Augustinian and Newtonian-mechanistic cosmologies and cultural frameworks, the former typically Roman Catholic; the latter Protestant.[10]

Torrance's theory is a fascinating one, but hardly convincing to a Catholic Luther scholar. Luther belongs, according to Torrance, to the dualistic deviation of the Western Christian tradition. Heidegger, to the contrary, repeatedly exempted Luther's theology from his otherwise all-out critique of the same tradition.[11] What Torrance sees as "dualism," "Luther's masterful distinction between 'the two kingdoms' of faith and sight, gospel and law, etc.,"[12] is, in fact, dialectical. Luther's dialectic discloses as irrelevant the very idea of a theology "in reconciliation." In Luther's eyes, theology is discontinuity, not on account of any cultural development, but simply because it has to hold to biblical revelation or else become meaningless. Torrance brings to light in modern terms a theological problematic that he shares with Luther: the conflict of the gospel with theological formulations and with behaviors originating in cultural patterns. He does this in a striking and illuminating way, but he also demonstrates that he himself is after the wrong solution, not only insofar as Luther is concerned, but also with regard to the future of Christian theology and the help it can expect from revolutions in the areas of culture and learning.

The real question then is what kind of break or discontinuity does Luther advocate? Gerhard Ebeling in his book *Luther: An Introduction to His Thought* approaches this question by studying Luther's famous conceptual oppositions: letter and spirit, law and gospel, person and work, and so on.[13] In his chapter on law and gospel, Ebeling establishes that Luther's theological method is above all the skill of correctly distinguishing what usually goes undistinguished.[14] By distinguishing between law and gospel, for example, Luther did not wish them to be absolutely separated; even less did he wish them to be reconciled.

According to Ebeling in the same chapter, Luther developed his method in view of a new hermeneutical interpretation of the word of God. But the issue here is not existential; it is logical. Luther's theological dialectic, whatever its unquestionable existential import, may have crystallized into later Protestant, "Newtonian," cosmological and epistemological dualism, as Torrance describes it. Yet it is not the mere "taking up of the epistemological, sacramental and cosmological dualism of Augustinianism into the Reformation . . . perpetuating a dualistic structure in Protestant society and culture."[15] Torrance's epistemological concerns lead him too far, and clearly away from Luther. In Luther's texts, the epistemological datum in the foreground is the paradigm of the Cross, as exemplified in 1 Cor. 1.[16] Christ's mystery is the actual basis for every dialectical venture of Luther's. This kind of dialectic has no possible development in terms of reconciliation, because it deals unremittingly with the irreconcilable. The key word in Luther's challenge to the Western Church's framework of thought and life is *sin*, a word that hardly fits into Torrance's reconciliation theory, centered on the integrative function of theology as a means toward establishing "a Christian reconstruction of the foundations of culture."[17]

There is little to be gained in a consideration of Luther's dialectic apart from its historical setting, that is, apart from the logic of a much-needed biblical and evangelical reaction to scholastic thought. Above all, Luther felt compelled to devise a way out of the Roman Catholic unchristological pattern of justification, and his new understanding of the Bible made him follow this logic. Ebeling seems to me to give a clue toward such an interpretation of Luther's theological achievement. In his paper at the Luther Congress in St. Louis in 1971, he insisted that Luther research should emphasize much more Luther's understanding of sin. He even added: "Isolated from the understanding of sin, Luther's reference to the modern age loses its specific character."[18] This is precisely what I too would assert. The more I understand Luther's concept of sin, the more I see his relationship with modern culture and learning, and, indeed, the meaning of his entire theology. For me

Luther has become the "Doctor of sin" who succeeded Augustine, the Doctor of grace. Grace characterizes the development of the Western Middle Ages; sin is the insight the Roman Church needed most as it entered into the modern age.

Sin in Luther's theology is much more than a moral issue. It is a logical element, the decisive element in Luther's theological method. Perhaps only a Catholic can fully value this fact. Jared Wicks reminds us that "Luther opened his exposition of Romans in 1515 by stating what he took to be the substance of Paul's message in the letter as a whole, namely, to pull down, to pluck out, and to destroy all human wisdom and carnal righteousness, so as to implant the reality of sin." And he continues: "This is a good instance of Luther's penchant for thought and expression in terms of opposed totalities. Luther communicated the biblical call for conversion through rhetorical schemes of dialectical opposition, in which contents stand in sharp discontinuity with each other. . . . Schooled as he was in Paul, especially in Gal 1–2 and 1 Cor 1, Luther found it second nature to highlight exclusive alternatives, oppositions brooking no compromise, and totalities set in discontinuity."[19]

Following Paul, Luther moved against human wisdom, together with denouncing carnal righteousness, "so as to implant the reality of sin." One must see in such a move, as early as the *Lectures on Romans* of 1515–1516, the very fact that accounts for Luther's "second nature," the Pauline highlighting of "exclusive alternatives, oppositions brooking no compromise, and totalities set in discontinuity." The most significant of such oppositions in Luther's theology seems to me to be grace and sin, which in more "cultural" terms is God and evil, a dialectic, not a dualism.

It is my experience in reading Luther in light of an intimate knowledge of Roman Catholicism that dictates these conclusions. Luther's dialectic is obviously in direct relationship to his reaction to the Roman Church. The authors I have cited usually fail to appreciate Luther's theories as an answer to the problems he discovered in the Catholicism of his times. All too often scholars explain Luther according to the Bible or a general conception of Christianity, Catholic or Protestant. The alternative that I follow is to understand most of his writings first and foremost on the basis of what is found in Roman Catholicism as such, in our times as well as in his, of what I would call grace positivism.

As medieval Catholicism developed Augustine's work toward a Church and a cultural framework converging on grace as a touchstone, more and more positivist conceptions of the various aspects of the doctrine of grace developed. In Luther's time even material objects were identified with grace, along with scholastic abstractions. Besides grace as a *habitus,* one had different kinds of so-called actual grace, and, for the ordinary Christian, relics, letters of indulgence, statues, and rosaries. By putting the emphasis on sin, Luther wanted to make it impossible to rely on human intellectual and cultural creations in order to take hold of divine grace. Instead of articulating the theology of grace according to human distinctions and fancies, he centered it on God himself, on the Word of God. Grace became for Luther a question about God: How do I find a gracious God? This perspective has remained quite foreign to the Catholic framework of thought and life up to our time. Roman Catholicism does not look at the crucified God as *the* grace that copes entirely with the issue of sin or evil. It continues to enjoy the possession of grace as a "treasure" from which to draw advantages, often enough material or cultural.

However, I did not quite understand Luther's sin-grace dialectic until I became interested in Theodor W. Adorno's writings, among them his book on the negative dialectic.[20] The idea of a "negative" dialectic opposes the common concept of dialectic as a method that allows one to find positive solutions to all possible contradictions. The best known example of this concept is Hegel's philosophy, in which the negative is overcome by being integrated into a further concept. Adorno's subtle discussions make one aware of how little interest our Western culture has given to the real import of the negative. Whatever the value of the Hegelian method or any other positive dialectic, the assimilation of the negative into the concept leads to totalitarian conceptual schemes, which can even generate totalitarian social systems.

Roman Catholicism reflects such a totalitarian pattern—the papal system, the dogmatic fixation of the Christian truth in a way that proves lethal to dissenters. Its "infallible" theology of grace lacks an appropriate apprehension of the negative. This is what Luther perceived, and what he wanted to correct with his new theology of the Cross.

Studying various major texts of Luther's, I am always under the impression that the Wittenberg reformer found himself already on the road that was to be that of Adorno centuries later.[21] Both of them feel compelled to dispute the most typical feature of Western thought, that is, the positivist abuse of reason, at two significant stages in the same cultural development: at the point of medieval theological learning, derived from Aristotelian grace positivism, and at that of secularized rationalist ideology from the Enlightenment.

In his *Dialektik der Aufklärung*, Adorno, together with Horkheimer, demonstrates that the secularization process has done away with religion without changing the basic concept of reason inherited from medieval Catholicism and fruitlessly opposed by Luther. Heidegger had already pointed out that the Aristotelian "onto-theological" framework of thought in the Western Church had passed unaltered into modern thought. Torrance writes of "causal connections," and "mechanical structures," features that one finds underlying the Roman Catholic system of grace.[22] What Adorno describes as "myth" was still, for Luther, religion. Luther discussed matters in theological terms because of the religious, cultural situation of which he was a part.

One finds the very same logical structures in Luther's theological and in Adorno's philosophical reaction to rationalism, religious or secular.[23] Luther opened the debate on the negative in the Western Christian cultural world at the outset of the modern age. It took centuries before modern thinkers came to the same realization that he had reached, that positivism is the real problem in Western culture and learning. Luther's insight had been long forgotten by Protestants while Catholics simply rejected Luther entirely.

In Luther's dialectic the negative element is sin, and it is precisely Catholic grace positivism that is thereby addressed. But Luther's negative dialectic is much more than merely religiously "colored." Compared with Adorno's theory, it avoids the deadlocks of a purely rational, negative dialectic, which seems unable to find a way toward a new positive synthesis while keeping the mind on the verge of despair. Adorno's aim is to recover the concreteness of the individual and of reality, but the result is invariably one of nihilism. Heidegger himself evolved from the "deconstruction" of metaphysics to the ineffable, resorting in the end to Hölderlin's hermetic language. Luther's negative dialectic, on the other hand, is decidedly theological; it is the dialectic of the Cross. This fact suggests that a negative dialectic can only be theological. By holding to the category of myth, Adorno omits any hint of the theological categories of revelation and faith, but in so doing he fails to take into account that Western rationalism is intrinsically of religious origin and suffers from this "original" sin, the estrangement of reason from the Christian faith, without which there never would have been a "Christian" culture in the West. Relying on the biblical teaching about sin, Luther, unlike Adorno, understands that the negative can in no way become the basis for any positive reconstruction. The negative can only be a critical element. It cannot be developed for its own sake, for the mere purpose of negating, nor be used toward attaining a new synthesis. The negative functions as a corrective, the means of breaking the yoke of any positivist system. Luther never implants sin as a value in itself, either for the sake of the individual or in order to express the real.[24] The negative upsets positivism for the benefit of the *positive*, without infringing upon it. On the contrary, the positive, grace, is brought fully into the light through the critic, the dialectic of sin.

These few observations about Luther's theological, negative dialectic remind us that the Roman Church has been the educator of the West and has for centuries shaped our Western culture into what it still is. Roman Catholicism was, already in the Middle Ages, the decisive fosterer of Western, modern conceptions and use of reason until the Church of Rome lost her leadership to later, cultural authorities. Luther reacted to Catholicism explicitly as the bearer of learning. He did not resist the papal system merely because of what seemed to him corrupt religious practices or distorted theological conceptions. His Reformation movement was also as such a contribution to learning proper. It challenged the authority that controlled the cultural sphere as well as the system of belief, and that favored scholastic rationalism under the pretense of faith. Issues such as justification, the knowledge of God, and the interpretation of evil were intertwined with purely cultural problems. They should not have been allowed to retreat into exclusive and unsolvable theological controversies.

The frightening experiences of the twentieth century have opened our eyes and minds. We now realize that Martin Luther's significance reaches far beyond ecclesiastical interests. Luther's contribution to learning points to issues that must be discussed today when our present critics of modernity are unable to suggest anything to replace a culture they unanimously condemn.

In conclusion, I wish to summarize what seems to me to be the lasting contribution of Luther to learning, in the context of a consideration of his challenge to Roman Catholicism as a cultural factor.

The most significant fact, in the light of the contemporary debate concerning rationalism, is Luther's introduction of a modern theory of the negative into our culture. The decisive importance of that kind of approach was rediscovered only during the time of Kant and Hegel, and repeatedly since then. For the modern age Luther constituted the first Enlightenment since he set the individual free from the obligation of accepting the words of his fellow human beings as his own thinking. The free Christian described by Luther thinks for himself—thinks critically. Beyond this contribution, Luther appears to have offered the possibility of quite another Enlightenment than that which occurred in the eighteenth century. Had Rome not condemned Luther's theses and had Protestants remained faithful to them, we might have had a completely nonpositivist development of modern rationality. What we are trying today to free ourselves from, Luther made it possible for us never to have entered into!

Luther's challenge to Catholicism reveals that learning is not a purely intellectual issue. The main problem is spiritual, as has become evident in this time when rational power, scientific or technological, makes the world more and more inhuman. Catholicism, followed by both humanism and the Enlightenment, has favored a strictly intellectual conception of learning, with boundless ambitions. In his Heidelberg Disputation of 1518 Luther made clear that purely rational knowledge misses the truth of God's revelation, perverts moral values, and serves human pretenses.[25] Thesis 24 gives the perfect description of the problem: "It is not that learning (*sapientia illa*) is bad . . . but man without the theology of the Cross abuses in the worst manner the best things."[26] Learning always needs a touch of the theology of the Cross in order not to degenerate into positivism, what Luther called *theologia gloriae,* or become the craft of the sorcerer's apprentice.

Luther also contended that learning, as a consequence of Adam's

fall, is subject to the might of evil, the evil forces.[27] Both Catholic
and modern optimism have unanimously rejected the alleged ex-
cesses of Luther in his 1525 treatise on the enslaved will. Our
culture, both religious and secular, will consider only the power of
human reason and will, even in a world threatened by the rivalry of
the superpowers! Luther saw much more clearly than we do that
man is dependent on powers mightier than he is. Luther called
them "God" and "Satan," and one should be grateful to Heiko A.
Oberman for having given us a book with the title *Luther: Mensch
zwischen Gott und Teufel.*[28] This idea, man between God and the
devil, offers a definition of our situation, the more our world and
culture spin out of control. Our learning does not help much, and
the new power of the computer makes us fear even more.

Our tragedy is fear, and learning cannot do much to remedy it. A
prominent French historian, Jean Delumeau, has recently published a substantial study on the topic of sin and fear in the Christian West from the thirteenth to the eighteenth century.[29] It offers
us the picture that Luther had before him. As a young Augustinian
monk he began by trying to cope with his fear before God, *coram
Deo*—his fear of hell—and he eventually arrived at the insight that
sin is the key to the whole problematic. Only faith in Christ re-
lieves us from sin—and fear. That message is as true today as it was
in Luther's time, and for the same reasons.

No political or ideological system, no theological message, no
existing religion, is able to free our world from the Devil's grip.
Fear generates the will to power, and the power of our fellow
humans feeds new fears. No learning in today's culture is able to
deal with this situation. Only Martin Luther seems to have given
real answers to this predicament, to the problems of a Christian
world. I am confident that in the future Luther research will succeed in bringing Luther back to the cultural problems that were his
and are still ours, and to which his theological, negative dialectic
still belongs.

NOTES

1. Joseph Lortz, *Die Reformation in Deutschland: Mit einem Nachwort von
Peter Manns,* 6th ed. 2 vols. in 1 (1939–40; Freiburg i. Br., 1982). In English *The
Reformation in Germany,* trans. Ronald Walls, 2 vols. (New York, 1968).

2. Otto Hermann Pesch, "Luthers theologisches Denken—eine katholische Möglichkeit?," *Die Neue Ordnung* 23 (1969): 1–19. See also his book *Gerechtfertigt aus Glauben: Luthers Frage an die Kirche* (Freiburg i. Br., 1982), 109–10.

3. Peter Manns, *Ketzer oder Vater im Glauben?* (Hannover, 1980). Otto Hermann Pesch, "'Ketzerfürst' und 'Vater im Glauben': Die seltsame Wege katholischer 'Lutherrezeption'," in *Weder Ketzer noch Heiliger: Luthers Bedeutung für den ökumenischen Dialog,* ed. Hans Friedrich Geisser (Regensburg, 1982), 123–74.

4. John Calvin did not tolerate the so-called Nicodemites, who followed Reformed teachings but continued to live outwardly as Catholics. Many Catholics, however, who remained faithful to the Roman Church were also impressed and moved by Luther's call for evangelical renewal. The pious bishop of Würzburg, Lorenz von Bibra, was such a person during 1518–1519, as perhaps was Erasmus until 1520.

5. Karl-Heinz zur Mühlen, *Reformatorische Vernunftkritik und neuzeitliches Denken: Dargestellt am Werk M. Luthers und Fr. Gogarten* (Tübingen, 1980).

6. Karl Barth gives an impressive account of the shift of Protestantism to humanism, beginning in the eighteenth century, in *Die protestantische Theologie im 19. Jahrhundert: Ihre Vorgeschichte und ihre Geschichte* (Zurich, 1947).

7. André Jacob offers a helpful overview and discussion of authors, works, problems, and doctrines in his *Introduction à la philosophie du langage* (Paris, 1976). Contemporary scientists are also questioning traditional views of reason. See, for example, Michel Cazenave, ed., *Science et conscience: Les deux lectures de l'Univers. Colloque international de Cordoue, 1–5 Oct. 1979* (Paris, 1980).

8. Thomas F. Torrance, *Theological Science* (Oxford, 1969).

9. Ibid., *Theology in Reconciliation* (London, 1975), 8.

10. Ibid., 267–93.

11. See the relevant excerpts in Richard Kearney and Joseph Steven O'Leary, eds., *Heidegger et la question de Dieu* (Paris, 1980), 313, 334, 335.

12. Torrance, *Theology in Reconciliation,* 43.

13. Gerhard Ebeling, *Luther: An Introduction to His Thought,* trans. R. A. Wilson (Philadelphia, 1972).

14. Eberhard Jüngel rates as highly as does Ebeling Luther's "Kunst des rechten Unterscheidens." See his "Luther und die Theologie der Gegenwart," in *Luther und die Theologie der Gegenwart: Referate und Berichte des Fünften Internationalen Kongresses für Lutherforschung Lund, Schweden 14.–20. August 1977,* ed. Leif Grane and Bernhard Lohse (Göttingen, 1980), 24ff. See also Jüngel's book *Zur Freiheit eines Christenmenschen: Eine Erinnerung an Luthers Schrift* (Munich, 1978), 20ff.

15. Torrance, *Theology in Reconciliation,* 43.

16. See Daniel Olivier, "Dieu caché, Dieu crucifié: Le statut épistémologique de la théologie d'après Luther," *Lumière et Vie* 158 (1983):51–63.

17. Torrance, *Theology in Reconciliation,* 271.

18. Gerhard Ebeling, "Luther and the Beginning of the Modern Age," in *Luther and the Dawn of the Modern Era: Papers for the Fourth International Congress for Luther Research,* ed. Heiko A. Oberman (Leiden, 1974), 39. He also writes: "He [Luther] broached anew the essentially Christian and discovered that this had been distorted just in the Christianized age." 37

19. Jared Wicks, "Justification and Faith in Luther's Theology," *Theological Studies* 44 (March 1983): 9.

20. Theodor W. Adorno, *Negative Dialektik*, 4th ed. (1966; Frankfurt a. M., 1973), and Theodor W. Adorno and Max Horkheimer, *Dialektik der Aufklärung: Philosophische Fragmente* (1944; Frankfurt a. M., 1969).

21. *Disputatio Heidelbergae Habita* (1518), WA 1:350–74; *Operationes in Psalmos* (1519–1521), WA 5: 598–608 (Ps. 22); *In ep. S. Pauli ad Galatas Commentarius* (1535), WA 40/1: 432–52 (Gal. 3:13), among many instances. Pierre Bühler deals extensively with the negative dialectic in his work *Kreuz und Eschatologie: Eine Auseinandersetzung mit der politischen Theologie, im Anschluss an Luthers theologia crucis* (Tübingen, 1981), 333–51.

22. Torrance, *Theology in Reconciliation*, 12 and passim, 46, 75, 77, 280.

23. Adorno and Horkheimer analyze the failure of the Enlightenment in terms in many ways consonant with Luther's critical discussion of the Catholicism of his times. Their aim was to contribute to the coming into existence of a world in which totalitarianism would be impossible. *Dialektik der Aufklärung*, ii. They objected to the increasing "administration" of nature and human society, in the same way that Luther objected to the Roman administration of the "means of grace." They held that critical thought should not retreat before the intangible idol of "progress" in the same way that Luther affirmed the existence of enduring sin *(peccatum manens)* over against the ideal of moral perfection. They lamented the Enlightenment's fall into positivism, "the myth of the so-called 'facts,'" and the identification of "intelligence" with hostility toward the spirit, in the same way that Luther rejected materialistic applications of the gospel and spiritless scholastic intellectualism. *Dialektik der Aufklärung*, ix. Adorno himself called the negative dialectic an "anti-system." *Negative Dialektik*, 10. And one can observe that Luther had *no* system. Many of his writings remind us of what Adorno gave as mere models for a negative dialectic in the third part of his book, 211–400. According to Leif Grane, "Luther regarded [his] books as deeds, and by no means collected, enduring statements." "The Image of Myth and Reality," in *Seven-Headed Luther: Essays in Commemoration of a Quincentenary 1483–1983*, ed. Peter Newman Brooks (Oxford, 1983), 245.

24. Luther's *Deus absconditus*, the God who operates *a contrario*, is a good example of how a negative concept can be a sound critic of positivist ideas without becoming a source of truth. This topic is connected with Luther's attempt to implant the reality of sin. If sin is not to be unreal, one must consider the "reverse side" of God *(posteriora dei, WA 1:362, 2)*, the crucified God. Luther does not mean this to be a better revelation or conception of God. Christ is the "door" *(Ego sum ostium, WA 1:362, 19)* to the knowledge of the Father, the knowledge of what the word "God" really means, that is, according to the Bible, the loving revealing of Himself in His triune mystery. This is exactly what one has to grasp if the word *grace* is to assume its full meaning.

25. WA 1:361–63 (theses 19–24).

26. WA 1:363, 25–26.

27. Theses *De Homine*, theses 22, 24, and 25: [Homo est creatura] "post lapsum vero Adae subiecta potestati diaboli, peccato et morti, utroque malo suis viribus insuperabili et aeterno. . . . Quibus stantibus pulcherrima illa et excellentissima res rerum, quanta est ratio post peccatum relicta, sub potestate diaboli tamen esse concluditur. Ut homo totus et omnis, sive sit rex, dominus, servus, sapiens, iustus, et quibus potest huius vitae bonis excellere, tamen sit et maneat peccati et mortis reus sub diabolo oppressus." Gerhard Ebeling, *Lutherstudien*, vol. 2: *Disputatio de homine*, pt. 1 (Tübingen, 1977), 19–21.

28. Heiko A. Oberman, *Luther: Mensch zwischen Gott und Teufel* (Berlin, 1982). Rather than describing Luther as a medieval prophet who brings the Middle Ages to an end, I am more impressed by his writings, his theology between God and the Devil, which Catholics now discover at a time when the godless world has grown demonic and can but expect a new prophet—another Luther.

29. Jean Delumeau, *Le Péché et la peur: La culpabilisation en Occident, XIII-XVIIIe siècles* (Paris, 1983).

6

THE WORD OF GOD AND THE WORDS OF LUTHER

Krister Stendahl
Bishop of Stockholm, Sweden

I offer my thoughts on the topic "The Word of God and the Words of Luther" in the spirit of the prayer of an old Hasidic rabbi: "One thing I ask of you, Lord, that I never use my reason against the truth."

To address this particular theme means that one must speak about Luther as a biblical scholar. Indeed, that was his primary occupation for some thirty-five years. He became a reformer in the very process of fulfilling his duties as a biblical scholar. One half of the material found in the American edition, *Luther's Works,* is comprised of commentaries and sermons, all biblical material.[1] In 1512, at the age of twenty-eight, Luther earned his doctorate *in Biblia.* And his famous last words, "Wir sein pettler. Hoc est verum,"[2] written in 1546, refer not to Christian existence in general but to how little of the riches of Scripture he had grasped.

I approach this topic not as a scholar of Luther, but as a scholar of the Bible, and as a scholar who was shaped in one of the most Lutheran of lands, Sweden. In confirmation class we were taught over and over again that the Reformation did not really succeed in Germany, but in Sweden, for there it was the one and only undivided church that was reformed. Thus I bring to this topic both my own experience as a biblical scholar and my Lutheran conscious-

ness. Both will inform my discussion of Luther as a biblical scholar
and theologian.

It is most appropriate to approach the theme of "Luther and
Learning" with a discussion of Luther as biblical scholar. Not only
was Luther himself first and foremost a scholar of the Bible, but
since his time, Lutherans have made a profound contribution to
biblical scholarship. To many people, and not only Lutherans,
when one asks who might be the leading figure in biblical studies
in our time, the name of Rudolf Bultmann comes immediately to
mind. Bultmann was himself so Lutheran that he translated the
term *justification by faith and not by works* into the statement
"justification by faith and not by historical knowledge," which
seemed to be a meaning appropriate to his time and concerns.
Thus both Luther himself and Lutheran biblical scholarship have
set their mark and stamp on the biblical field in many ways.

As I reflect on Luther the biblical scholar, I am repeatedly struck
by his multifaceted fascination with the word. As an educated and
lively mind of the early sixteenth century, Luther was part of the
Renaissance, and of the humanist movement. Luther shared the
humanists' excitement in returning to the sources, *ad fontes,* and
in their interest in texts, languages, and grammar. Luther often
called his own biblical method grammatical, and when it suited
him, it is amazing how much he could deduce from grammar.

Luther was one of many who found power and truth in *re*forma-
tion and *re*naissance, that is, in the belief that by returning to the
beginnings one would be closer to the truth. To many people such
a view seems obvious. On second thought, however, we may question whether it is really so self-evident. Is it not possible that the
church might have learned something new in the course of its
history? Is it not possible that some wisdom has emerged through
the faithful lives of generations of Christians? We tend implicitly by
our method to answer these questions in the negative. We continue to see ourselves as the people of the Reformation. We seek to
return to the origin, the pure truth that was in the beginning. This
idea, the notion that the original or beginning is the truth, has
carried with it an enormous legacy in our intellectual habits and
theological traditions. I would call it "the genetic fallacy." The
assumption is that if we know how things were in the beginning,
then we know the essence, everything worth knowing. Thus all

development is in fact a falling away. This is the way some Lutheran scholars, who still carry considerable animus against Catholicism, label that which they do not like in the New Testament. They call it *Frühkatholizismus*, incipient Catholicism, the apostasy from or at least the pollution of the true and original. Luther himself did not think in precisely those terms about the origin or beginnings of Christianity, but it is important to note that the fascination with returning to the sources, to the origin, to the pure, has had a mighty impact on our way of thinking and has left us with an intellectual model of great import in our culture.

As I read Luther the biblical scholar, I am continually fascinated and overwhelmed by his trust in the Word. When he spoke about the Word, he did not primarily think about grammar, but about the power of the Word. It was Luther who wrote about the Devil in his famous hymn: "One little word shall slay him." His grammatical method yields, quite rightly, the insight that the Hebrew *dabar* means both word and thing, both word and act. The word is act. Indeed, God created by speaking. The Word must have been an overwhelming experience for Luther in a time when much was happening to "words." With the invention of the printing press there was a new, popular interest in words and in translating the biblical languages into the vernacular. Luther was part of a time in which there was a new awareness of the word, and the power of language, in all sorts of contexts.

So powerful was Luther's emphasis on the Word that one can describe his relationship with it as a love affair. So intense is this love that it leads to the strange habit of calling the sacrament "the visible word."[3] The word has power and connotations. For Luther the word was not primarily the Word in the book or the Word canned in the canon, but the Word preached, the Word of proclamation. The powerful Word does things; indeed, it creates. The proclaimed Word shares in the power of the Word that God spoke when the entire cosmos sprang into being. As Isaiah describes it, the Word of God does not return to God without having accomplished its purpose (55:11). Luther spoke of the synagogue as a book house and the early church as the "mouth house,"[4] a house filled with the spoken Word, the proclamation of the gospel. It is the task of those who study the sixteenth century to ponder the sociological and psychological basis for this enormous fascination with the Word, but I dare attest to the fact that we can speak of the Reformation period as witnessing a "word explosion."

Luther was infatuated with the power of the Word, with the Word as message, with the Word as it relates to us individually and communally. There is an important and enlightening passage in Luther's 1525 sermon "How Christians Should Regard Moses" where he declares that there are two kinds of words, those that are for us and those that are not for us.[5] God said many things to David, but he did not say them to or for us. Luther remarked that his opponents kept repeating: "It is the word of God; it is the word of God; it is the word of God!" He responded by saying, "Yes, but not for me." Luther's basis for making this decision is rather interesting. He draws a distinction between material in the Scriptures that has proof value and material that is illustrative—a truly perceptive observation. In more modern terms, we may say that the very subsidiary arguments that speakers or writers employ are ancillary to their main point, and therefore their proof value is limited and of low density.[6] We must ask, of course, how Luther was able to distinguish between proof and illustration. Indeed, Luther himself could never present a convincing argument to justify his belief, but he trusted in the Word itself, in the power of the Word to steer matters right. Luther's criterion for deciding between proof and illustration was the Word as proclamation.

Luther perceived a compelling analogy between what he saw to be the human predicament and the message of the Scriptures. He believed justification by faith to be the answer for the troubled conscience, and certainly this sensitive man knew well the anguish of the conscience. According to Luther, the Bible is about this very anguish of the conscience and its need for comfort. The Bible answers the question: How can I find a gracious God? Luther had the audacity to claim that the whole Scripture centers around the issue of law and gospel, sin and forgiveness, the perception of the individual as *simul iustus et peccator,* at the same time righteous and a sinner. Because of Luther's own agonizing experience of sin, his words about grace and justification take on such intensity. Just as Paul said in a different context, Luther too affirmed that when sin increases, God's grace shines all the more (Rom. 5:20).

For Luther it seemed self-evident that Paul spoke about the struggle of the individual plagued by the demands of a law he could not fulfill. For Paul in Romans the issue was God's mysterious plan for the incorporation of the Gentiles into the People of God. It is important to note that Paul made it quite clear that this principle of *felix culpa* is singularly unsuited to the problems of the individual. For in Romans 6, where the problems of the individual are discussed, Paul shifts to a totally different language. In that context baptism as death is the answer, and there is no mention of justification by faith.

Once Luther had decided what constitutes the center of Scripture, all else came to serve that one central theme. Thus, whether he spoke of Pharisees or Jews, Papists, Turks, or Anabaptists, they were really all the same since it seemed to Luther that they all sought to attain righteousness in their own way, through works, without recognizing that righteousness is a divine gift. He saw them all as part of the drama that is the key to the Scriptures. Luther's Paul is the hero of Lutherans—and so everything else becomes negative background, and the more negative, the more his Paul shines.

When Luther had so defined the center of Scripture, everything else opened up in a new way. This is what we may term the adversary or oppositional structure in Luther's exegesis. It is understandable then that one of the super-Lutheran exegetes of our time, Ernst Käsemann, has suggested that the Holy Spirit is a polemicist by nature! In such a view it is in a consistently oppositional structure that the depth of theology emerges. Heiko Oberman has recently pointed to this dimension of Luther's theology in his book *Luther: Mensch zwischen Gott und Teufel.*[7] In Luther's biblical theology there is an adversary relationship toward everything that does not express the center of his theology. For example, when Luther wrote his introduction to the Psalms, he actually used it to offer a critique of saints' lives. From Luther's exegesis we emerge with this sense of him as a fighter. His entire structure of theology, of exegesis, his perception of the early church, is grounded in this adversary or oppositional viewpoint. In distinction to that perception, we must ask whether or not Jesus himself thought in such terms, or whether Jesus thought the most important ideas were those he held in common with some of the sages of his time, allowing for discussion on certain points. If we follow Luther, we perceive the essence of Jesus to be where he differed from other teachers. Many people in the women's movement would say that this is a typically male view of reality. The adversary nature of the entire Lutheran enterprise, when it has become glorified into an entire way of viewing reality, has had grave consequences and high costs.

The compelling and mighty analogy that Luther saw between his own religious problem and the problems of his time, on the one hand, and Scripture, on the other, led to what we may term a canon within the canon. The criterion for what qualified as Christian proclamation was defined in so-called Pauline terms. Other statements were considered either to be nonapostolic or merely illustrative of the center. Luther's great insight also leads to a de facto narrowing of the canon.

I am aware that I have spoken critically of Luther's insight, but I am also aware that little can be attained in this world without cost. What Luther contributed was a new and powerful clarity, a new language, a new magnet for the whole understanding of faith and Scripture. This magnet drew the scriptural texts—the metal filings—into a new, beautiful, and clear configuration. This powerful clarity about the central message of Scripture led to new energy not only in biblical study, but also in the life of the church and in the lives of millions.

Yet three questions remain to be asked, the first of which is really a series of questions. Can we be sure that Luther perceived the matter correctly? Is he correct in saying that the entire Bible circles around the question of sin and guilt? Can we be certain that the inner center of Scripture is truly justification by faith? If not, Luther's exegesis makes little sense. I am always puzzled by the fact that many of Paul's epistles do not make a single reference to justification by faith. Paul finds that the problems at hand demand other solutions in other language. He speaks then in very different terms of such matters: of the church as the body of Christ, and of love—not as overtly the love of God, but as the love Paul himself needed to have when writing to the glossolalia-obsessed Corinthians.

Why, then, did Paul not know his own theology and do what a Lutheran would do, namely, speak to the Corinthians, for example, about justification by faith? Perhaps then the Bible is really about something quite different from that which Luther defined as its center. Perhaps it is the story of how God is trying to mend the creation. Perhaps Jesus spoke of the kingdom, because, of the terms at his disposal, this one was best suited to the idea that God wishes to mend the creation. Thus, Jesus healed the sick, fed the hungry, and raised the dead—never old people but young ones who had died too early, since Jesus knew that death at the right time is not sad but belongs to the course of nature. Perhaps then the biblical world includes other concerns than those discussed by Luther, and perhaps the search for a "center," *the* message, is an arrogant enterprise.[8]

At the same time, we must agree that a tremendous burst of creative and healing energy emerged through Luther's teaching. We can still hear Luther saying to us: "You do not need to spend any of your energy on your own salvation; leave that in God's hands." Indeed, Luther affirmed that one can say this even if God consigns one to hell, because salvation consists in events happening according to God's plans and wishes. What Luther means by this statement, his affirmation of the *resignatio ad infernum,* is the possibility of a new and wonderful style of life where one is free of the preoccupation with one's own ego. That is what constitutes the freedom of a Christian for Luther, as he outlined it in his 1520 treatise.[9] Certainly this message has great meaning for us when we are obsessed with our own egos, when we devote ourselves to self-help and self-improvement techniques, as the present flood of popular literature on these subjects demonstrates.

Second, Luther was fascinated by the explosion of the word, vernacular, preached with clarity, printed, and proclaimed. He saw that it worked. But what about the Lutheran preoccupation with the Word in our world of word processors, in a world that suffers from an inflation of proclamations, where people are bombarded constantly by words? There was a time when the word spoken from the pulpit had a sanctity in and of itself; that time is gone. Is there, then, a flaw in Luther's understanding when we perceive that his high experience of the Word is rooted in a definite, cultural setting? Is it possible that much of the language of theology no longer works the way it did in Luther's day? Is it possible that we should now say: And the Word became flesh, and dwelt amongst us, and we saw—not heard—it?

Third, the major insight of contemporary biblical theology is the recognition that from the beginning of the Christian movement there was a diversity of theologies. The very essence of the early church was its diversity. Paul was only one among many teachers and preachers. We must then ask also for that reason: Is it wise to create a canon within the canon? Is it really so clear that the Scriptures witness to a certain *proclamation* at their center? I have always been skeptical of the so-called kerygmatic or proclamation theology. Peter, returning home from his fishing and his meeting with Jesus, did not stand on a chair and proclaim the gospel to his wife and mother-in-law. I suspect that he sat at the table and told what had happened that day. The pompous notion of preaching as proclamation has had ill effects on both pastors and congregations in recent times. Indeed, one Lutheran biblical scholar, Martin Dibelius, even went so far as to coin the phrase: *In the beginning was the sermon.* I find that to be an extreme example of the Lutheran projection of its dreams onto the world of the early church. Actually, contrary to the notion of Scripture as proclamation, the words that are collected in the Gospels seem to have been gathered there because they gave answers to specific questions and problems in the daily life of the community. The Gospels are much more stories and *halakha* than they are proclamation.

These are questions that modern biblical scholarship leads us to raise, not to mention our reappraisal of the stereotypical and ahistorical pictures of Pharisees and Jews that abound in Luther's works and that are part of his oppositional mode of theology.

The diversity of theologies suggests that the biblical model is one of complementarity rather than of opposition. The complementarity model may offer us more. Paul presents something very different from John. The two resist easy homogenization, and that is precisely what makes the Scriptures so rich. Therefore it seems to me that the most questionable inheritance we have from the biblical scholar Luther is his narrowing of Scripture, his creating of a canon within a canon, for the Word of God cannot be narrowed. Luther was a great enough biblical scholar to recognize that fact. He had many questions about aspects of the Bible that he did not think were good or appropriate. We think immediately of his problems with the Epistle of James, but he retained it in the Bible. Indeed, Luther even said that at times scriptural passages that he had not earlier seen as helpful suddenly came to his aid. Thus we must give thanks both for Luther's marvelous arrogance in achieving a clarity that released a new spiritual energy and a new perception of the meaning of the Word of God, and for his humility in allowing the Word of God to stand in its fullness, so that those of us who came after him might not be impoverished. And so his great spiritual insights can now play in a much wider ecumenical world than was his. As the lover of the Scriptures he was, I wonder if he does not like that fact—grudgingly or perhaps even gladly.

NOTES

1. *Luther's Works*, 55 vols. General editors: Jaroslav Pelikan, vols. 1–30; Helmut T. Lehmann, vols. 31–55 (St. Louis and Philadelphia, 1955–1976).

2. *WA TR* 5:318, 2–3, no. 5677; *Luther's Works*, vol. 54: *Table Talk*, ed. and trans. Theodore G. Tappert (Philadelphia, 1967), 476.

3. See Jaroslav Pelikan, *Luther's Works, Companion Volume: Luther the Expositor. Introduction to the Reformer's Exegetical Writings* (St. Louis, 1959), 219–36.

4. *WA* 10/1²: 48, 5 (*Adventspostille* 1522). See also Pelikan, *Luther the Expositor,* 62–64.

5. *WA* 16:383–88; *Luther's Works*, vol. 35: *Word and Sacrament I*, ed. E. Theodore Bachmann (Philadelphia, 1960), 169–72.

6. On the density discussion, see my article "Preaching from the Pauline Epistles," in James W. Cox, ed., *Biblical Preaching* (Philadelphia, 1983), 306–13.

7. Heiko A. Oberman, *Luther: Mensch zwischen Gott und Teufel* (Berlin, 1982).

8. See the chapter "One Canon is Enough" in my volume *Meanings* (Philadelphia, 1984), 55–68.

9. *WA* 7:49–73; *Luther's Works*, vol. 31: *Career of the Reformer: I*, ed. Harold J. Grimm (Philadelphia, 1957), 343–77.

INDEX OF NAMES